FORTIFIED

From Fear, Anxiety, and Bondage
to Freedom and Power in Jesus

Jim Stern

Published by Trexo
Houston, Texas

Fortified: From Fear, Anxiety, and Bondage to Freedom and Power in Jesus

© 2015 by Jim Stern

All rights reserved. No portion of this workbook may be reproduced, stored in a retrieval system, or transmitted in any form or by any means (electronic, mechanical, photocopy, recording, scanning, or other) except for brief quotations in critical reviews or articles, without the prior written permission of the publisher.

Published in Houston, Texas by Trexo.

Edited by Blake Atwood with EditFor.me.

Unless otherwise noted, Scripture quotations are taken from the New American Standard Bible®, © The Lockman Foundation 1960, 1962, 1963, 1968, 1971, 1972, 1973, 1975, 1977, 1995. Used by permission.

For more resources by Trexo, visit www.trexo.org.

CONTENTS

Foreword V

1: The Reality of War 1

2: The City of Jerusalem 5

3: Enemies 13

4: The City of You 27

5: Freedom 45

Appendix 1: List of Sins 69

Appendix 2: Names God Calls Me 71

Appendix 3: Freedom Worksheet 73

Further Reading 79

About the Author 81

FOREWORD

"It was for freedom that Christ set us free; therefore keep standing firm and do not be subject again to a yoke of slavery." The Apostle Paul, Galatians 5:1

According to Paul there is a difference between being set free and staying free. The purpose of this book is to help followers of Jesus learn how to be set free. In *FORTIFIED*, you will learn the three sources of bondage, the four primary places where attack happens, and how to be freed by the love and power of the Father, Son, and Holy Spirit.

The great reality for humanity is that because of Jesus there is always hope. No power, force, person, or gathering of people (even nations) is stronger than Jesus. Psalm 2:1–3 envisions a scenario where all the nations and armies of the world are gathered together against the Lord and His Anointed. Verse 4 records God's response: "He who sits in the heavens laughs, the Lord scoffs at them." Can you picture the scene? God is laughing at the arrogance of man who thinks they have some possible way of overcoming Him. He laughs.

In the same way, powers and forces are actively working to overcome Christ in you. When we can identify what or who they are and where they have attacked, we are much better positioned to see them and be freed from.

Once freed, we need to live in relationship with the Father, Son, and Holy Spirit in a way that maintains our promised freedom. Staying free is different than getting free. Paul trains the Philippian disciples in Philippians 4:9, "The things you have learned and received and heard and seen in me, practice these things, and the God of peace will be with you."

Paul had a particular way of being a disciple of Jesus that kept him free in the peace of God. Liberated from bondage, we need to learn a way of being a disciple of Jesus that will keep us free. I wrote the book *Be: The Way of Rest, A Holistic Recipe for Walking With Jesus* to provide followers of Jesus a recipe that works. Anyone who embraces The Way of Rest as their recipe will experience the clarity, confidence, and promises God intended all His children to know. If you do not have clarity and confidence in your relationship with Jesus, if you do not know how to live free, then I highly encourage you to read *Be: The Way of Rest* when you are done with *FORTIFIED*.

May your eyes be opened to all the Holy Spirit wants to show you through this work.
You are not alone. There is hope in Jesus.

THE REALITY OF WAR

Life is war. To live is to be under constant attack from within and from without. You live in fear of losing your job, not having enough money to support your family, failing as a spouse or a parent. You are cheating on your spouse or about to cheat either physically or emotionally. You are trapped in the dark hell of pornography. You struggle with your spouse's chronic illness. You have a chronic illness.

All part of the war.

You feel like you wander aimlessly. Does your life really matter? You are burning your life trying to please a parent you are never going to please. You bear the internal wounds of getting the stuff kicked out of you at home. You have wasted half your life and blown up every relationship you have because you cannot stop your addiction. You live in an internal spin cycle of anxiety, stress, fear, pride, instability, anger, jealously, gossip, rage, lust, selfishness, and self-pity. You live on anti-depressants and anti-anxiety medications but are still depressed and anxious.

You see injustice, fraud, greed, lies, deception, and immorality in most places: government, education, business, and even religion. You watch the news and see war, disease, sickness, murder, natural disasters, riots, and more.

This is the war.

Some were awakened to the war early in life. Some came to this reality as the idealism of youth gave way to the harshness of adulthood. Others choose to live in denial all the while suffering the hits and bearing the marks. Others are semi-awake to it but are severely confused as to what is going on.

Take some heart: it is not just you. It is everyone. Everywhere. You don't have to be a psychologist or a psychiatrist to know this. Talk to people. Ask them how they are doing. Get past the superficial, "I'm doing fine," to the reality of life. It is not pretty.

There are real persons and real forces at work in life who actively, aggressively, and systematically seek to rob you of your life. They are masters of subtlety, deceit, and blending in.

A security expert was hired to test the security of a major store. Unknown to the store manager, the security expert entered the store one day and began stealing thousands of dollars in merchandise. No one stopped him! After stealing toys, clothes, and a television, he decided to steal the most outlandish item possible: a bike.

He rode the bike in the store, past an employee at the door, into the parking lot, and loaded it in the back of his van. When the security expert told the store manager what he had done, the store manager said it was impossible and claimed he was lying. The security expert showed the store manager the merchandise. He was speechless! The store manager was in denial that his store's goods were being stolen.

Similarly, too many of us live in denial that our lives are being stolen, that we live in captivity.

In His time, Jesus dealt with various groups of Jews who were blind to the war they were in and their own captivity.

> So Jesus was saying to those Jews who had believed Him, "If you continue in My word, then you are truly disciples of Mine; and you will know the truth, and the truth will make you free." They answered Him, "We are Abraham's descendants and have never yet been enslaved to anyone; how is it that You say, 'You will become free'?" (John 8:31–33).

This is an incredible exchange between Jesus and a group of Jews. He offers freedom if they will follow Him. He does not offer them freedom if they follow a religion. He offers them freedom if they will enter into a relationship—an active, ongoing, dynamic relationship with Him.

For the time being, separate everything you know, think you know, and have seen about Christianity, from walking in a tight, deep, living, on-going relationship with Jesus. As unfortunate as it is, a planetary-wide gulf has developed between a lot of Christianity and walking with Jesus. In this passage, Jesus is not talking about a religion or a denomination. His offer of freedom comes from Him.

Incredibly, the Jews respond that they, being Abraham's descendants, have never been enslaved to anyone. No one has ever stolen their lives. The Jews' response is . . . laughable.

This conversation happened somewhere between 27–30 AD. The Jews had lived in some form of captivity since the Assyrians sacked the northern kingdom in 722 BC. Since then, the Jews were passed from Assyria to Babylon to Persia to Greece and finally to Rome. Even before captivity to the Assyrians, the Israelites spent 400 of their nation's formative years in slavery to Egypt! To say that they have "never yet been enslaved to anyone" puts a bizarre spin on the definition of freedom. (I would have liked to see the look on Jesus's face when they said they had never been enslaved.)

I am writing this because, like the Jews of John 8, there is rampant confusion among Christians and non-Christians about the freedom and restoration Jesus offers. **Jesus came to set people free.** It was a primary part of His mission. Luke 4:16–18 is considered part of Jesus's mission statement. Quoting Isaiah 61:1–2, Jesus says:

> The Spirit of the Lord is upon Me,
> Because He anointed Me to preach the gospel to the poor.
> He has sent Me to proclaim release to the captives,
> And recovery of sight to the blind,
> To set free those who are oppressed,
> To proclaim the favorable year of the Lord (Luke 4:18–19).

Jesus's mission to free people is seen in John 8, here in Luke 4, and in many other teachings and stories of Jesus.

You have great hope in this war because of Jesus.

Jesus gives you reason to believe, reason to live, reason to celebrate, and reason to reach others. Only in Jesus can you be freed. And only in Jesus can you stand strong no matter the size of the weapon pointed at you.

Jesus's disciples picked up His mission. Paul writes in Galatians 5:1, "It is for freedom that Christ set us free; therefore keep standing firm and do not be subject again to a yoke of slavery." Peter writes in 1 Peter 2:16–17, "Act as free men, and do not use your freedom as a covering for evil, but use it as bondslaves of God. Honor all people, love the brotherhood, fear God, honor the king." Freedom is a work of Jesus in those who follow Him.

The promise of freedom was not limited to the New Testament. One of the most powerfully worded promises of God's freeing work is found in Joel 2:25, "I will restore to you the years that the swarming locust has eaten . . ."(ESV). Psalm 107 is one of many powerful psalms of deliverance and freedom. From the fall of Adam to the return of Jesus, God has moved to free His people.

God's people should be living free lives.

Unfortunately, many Christians respond like the Jews: "We are Christians and do not live in slavery." But their lives do not demonstrate freedom. They are equally bound up in fear, insecurity, anxiety, pride, selfish ambition, deceit, and anger as those who do not know Jesus. Where is the freedom? Where is the life? Where is the Free Army rising up to set others free?

Then there are Christians who want freedom but are confused and frustrated because they can't find answers. The things they have been doing are not working. They live in what is called the "tortured middle," the wasteland between denying Jesus and living in His promises.

So then what do those without Christ see? Lives they would not want to live. They do not see an answer. They see no hope!

I am writing this, *praying* that the Holy Spirit will use this simple tool to help you get free. I am writing this to offer clarity and understanding so that the free can be mobilized to go and help others find freedom. I expect that anyone who walks through this will have a new opportunity to be loosed from exhausting, debilitating burdens. The loosening will be met with a new depth of intimacy with the Father, Son, and Holy Spirit. If your freedom does not come with intimacy with God then it is no freedom. Finally, I expect this freedom and intimacy to propel followers of Jesus to go and help others breathe the same pure air that free people breathe.

Are you ready to deal with your issues?
Are you ready to live free?
Let's get to work.

THE CITY OF JERUSALEM

We are going to learn about freedom and restoration by looking at God's restoration of Jerusalem. Jerusalem provides a great example of God's construction, destruction, and restoration. The Temple, walls, gates, and land of the city will give us a working picture of who we are and how God's restoration works.

This should be simple enough to be powerfully used in bringing restoration to anyone who wants it. Knowing the history of God's work in Jerusalem is important as it will give you insight into how God works to free us. Additionally, Jerusalem's history will help you anchor God's restorative work today to what He has always been doing.

God is the God of freedom and restoration.

Under the leadership of King David, Jerusalem became the capital of the fledgling Israelite people around 1000 BC. The city was already surrounded by a wall. The wall gave Jerusalem an identity.

Defining the boundaries of the city, the wall said, "THIS IS JERUSALEM." Additionally, the wall provided defense. In a time when invading armies were normal, a city with a wall had an ability to defend itself against attackers. A strong city needed a strong wall.

Built into the wall were a series of gates. In David's time there were three. (Later, in the time of Nehemiah, there were ten.) The gates functioned to control who came in and out of the city. The leaders could, at any time, deny access to anyone. A strong gate system was an important component to a strong city.

King David wanted to build a grand Temple to God, His home in the midst of His people. However, God gave this work to David's son and heir to his throne, Solomon. Solomon completed the Temple in 952 BC.

The Temple had three sections: The Outer Court, the Holy Place, and the Holy of Holies. The Outer Court was open to all Jews, a common area. The Holy Place had limited access; only the priests could enter. The Holy of Holies was further limited. Only the High Priest could enter, and he could only enter once a year.

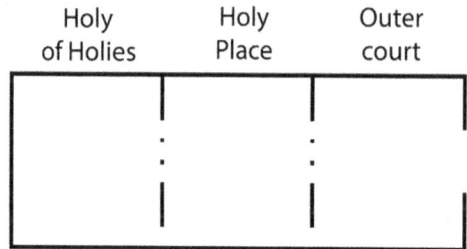

Figure 1: A rough approximation of the Temple

It is in the Holy of Holies where the presence of God literally was in the Ark of the Covenant. God could now be as close to His people as possible. He wanted intimacy and nearness—the Holy of Holies was designed to be that place. The Holy of Holies was the deepest part of the Temple, and consequently the deepest part of the identity of the Israelite people. God's Temple presence was the essence, the core, of Jerusalem and of all Israel. Upon completion God came and filled the Temple with His presence:

> Then the house, the house of the Lord, was filled with a cloud, so that the priests could not stand to minister because of the cloud, for the glory of the Lord filled the house of God (2 Chronicles 5:13–14).

God's presence in the Temple differentiated Jerusalem from every other city on earth. Now the city could say:

WE ARE JERUSALEM, THE CITY OF GOD.

Needless to say, Israel took great comfort and strength from God's presence. It was the center of their national worship and identity.

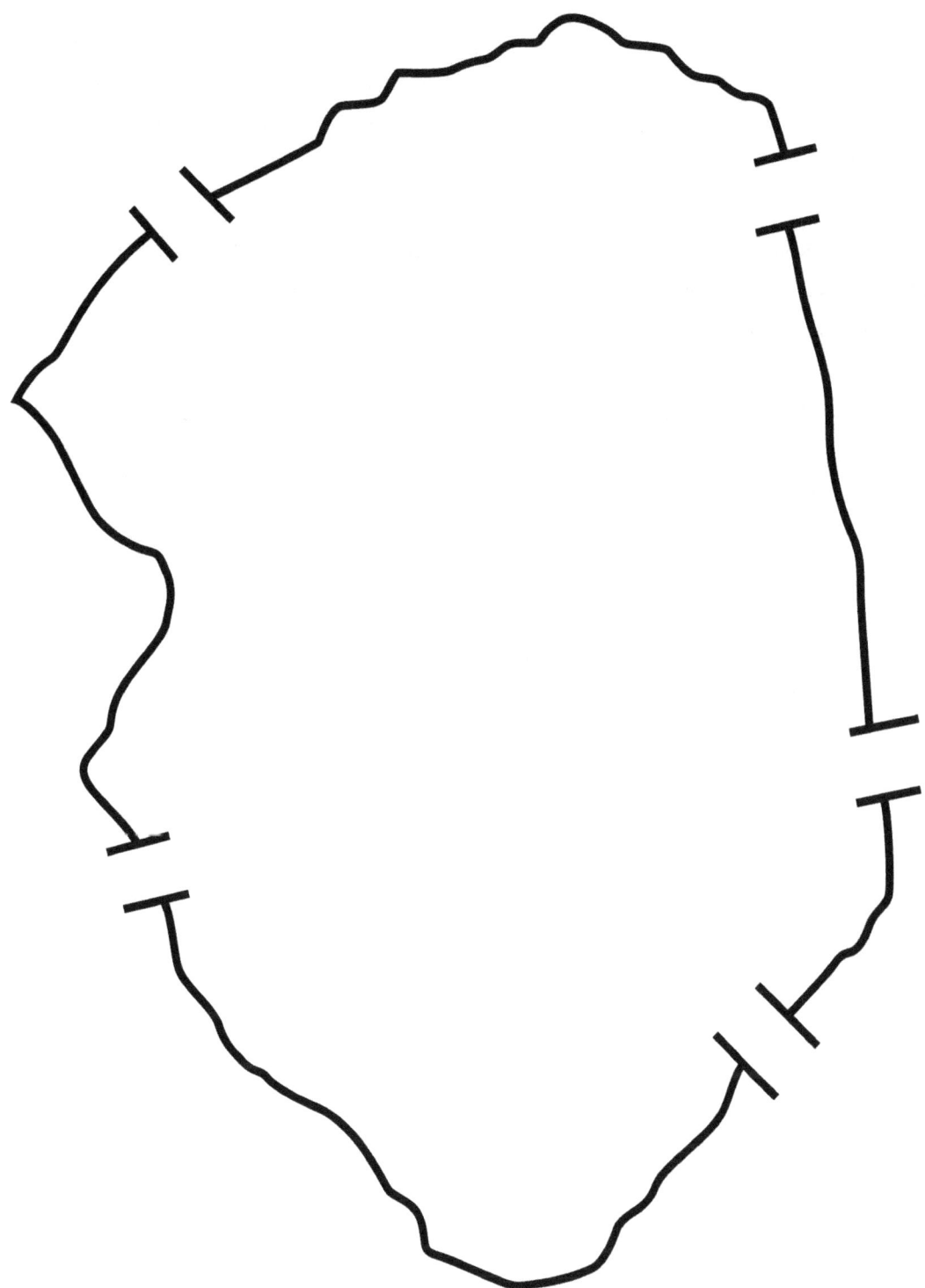

Figure 2: A representation of Jerusalem with a wall and a gate

The Fall of Jerusalem

God led His people to build Jerusalem such that it would be a "city on a hill" shining the Light of His revelation to the world. He intended the people in the city to live in holiness out of their love for Him and His ways. Jerusalem was to be a city unlike any other populated by people unlike any other. It was to be magnificent.

Unfortunately, Jerusalem shined only for a brief time. The Israelites took God for granted and brought sin inside their walls. They forsook God and His ways. The city, intended to be a refuge to the world, became a place of rebellion. The prophet Isaiah said:

> How the faithful city has become a harlot,
> She who was full of justice!
> Righteousness once lodged in her,
> But now murderers.
> Your silver has become dross,
> Your drink diluted with water.
> Your rulers are rebels
> And companions of thieves;
> Everyone loves a bribe
> And chases after rewards.
> They do not defend the orphan,
> Nor does the widow's plea come before them (Isaiah 1:21–23).

While in decline from its peak during Solomon's reign, Jerusalem would not be devastated until 587 BC. Because of their sin, God raised up the nation of Babylon to lay waste to Jerusalem. In 587 BC, the Babylonian king Nebuchadnezzar led his army against the hallowed city. In a siege that lasted three years, Jerusalem fell.

Not only did the Babylonians destroy the wall, but they also demolished the Temple, taking all of the sacred objects back to Babylon. In line with Babylonian foreign policy, they also deported all of the Israelites to Babylon to be integrated into their way of life. The future of Jerusalem, God's chosen city, seemed bleak.

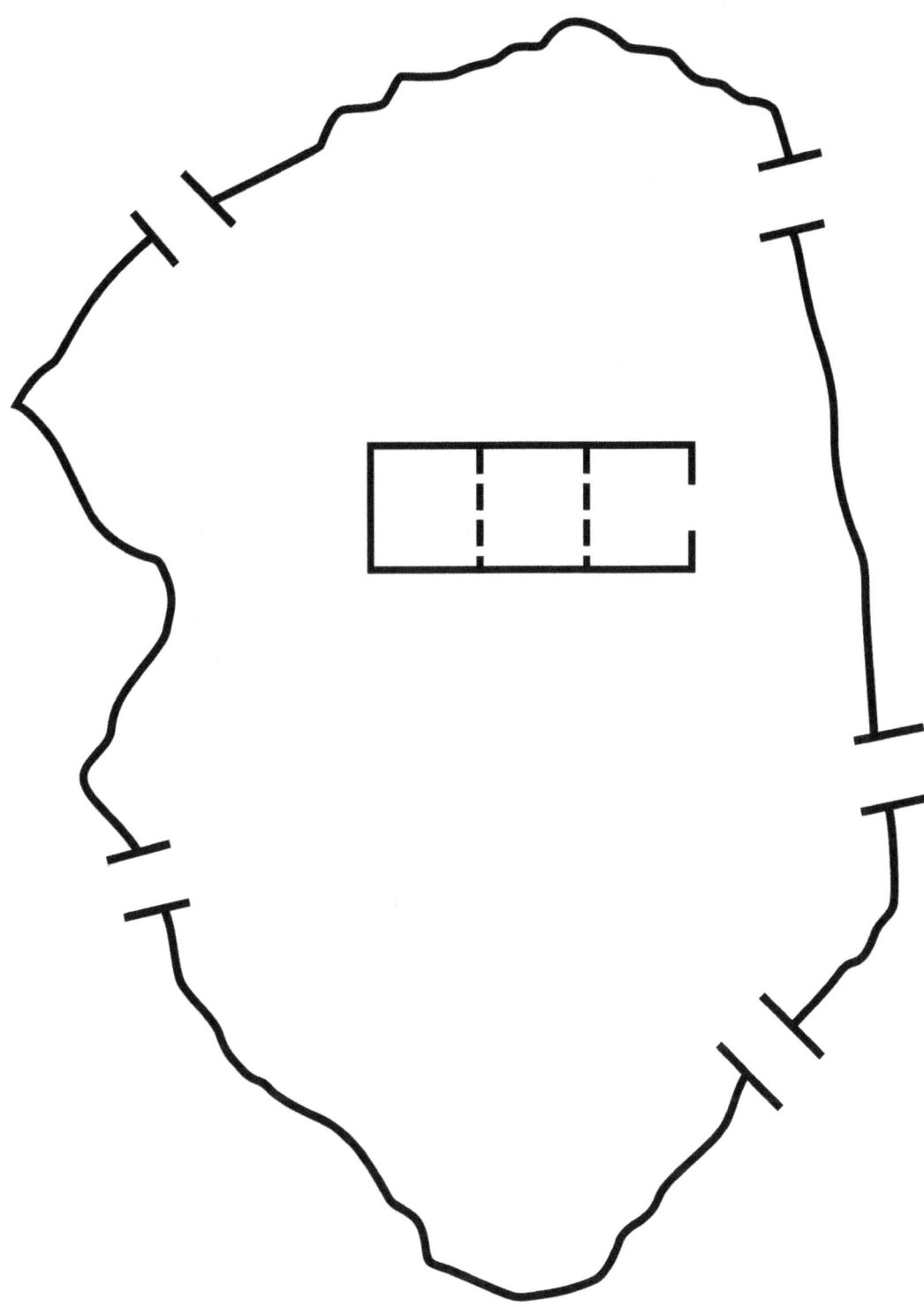

Figure 3: Jerusalem with its Temple, walls, gates, and land.

Jerusalem Restored

However, even in the absolute darkness of destruction brought on by sin, God's restoration was still possible. His prophet Jeremiah predicted Israel's captivity would last 70 years (Jeremiah 25:11). In 539 BC, Nabonidus, the king of Babylon, was defeated by Cyrus, the king of the ascendant Media-Persian Empire.

The Persian's foreign policy differed from the Babylonian's. Under Persian policy, the Jews were allowed to return to rebuild their city. How would God rebuild Jerusalem? What would He do first? Would Jerusalem ever attain its God-intended fullness?

According to Ezra 3:1–9, two men named Jeshua and Zerubbabel rebuilt the Temple.

The first step in restoration is to rebuild the Temple.

Before the walls and gates, God moves to rebuild the Temple. This makes sense because God's great desire is intimacy with His people. The God of all creation has always wanted intimacy with His people.

As is the case in God's restorative work, there was opposition to the rebuild. There are always those who do not want to see God's work done. Ezra 4 details different schemes the opponents used to try and stop what God was doing. Jeshua and Zerubbabel stood strongly against them.

The second step in restoration is to reject opposition.

In spite of fierce opposition, the Temple was completed in 516 BC! God will finish His work.

The third step in restoration is to rebuild the gates and the wall.

Following the building of the Temple, God raised up Nehemiah to return from Babylon and rebuild the city's gates and wall. Like Jeshua and Zerubbabel, Nehemiah faced great opposition. Two men, Sanballat and Tobiah, warred against the restoration. Nevertheless, Nehemiah's work was completed.

> So the wall was completed on the twenty-fifth of the month Elul, in fifty-two days. When all our enemies heard of it, and all the nations surrounding us saw it, they lost their confidence; for they recognized that this work had been accomplished with the help of our God (Nehemiah 6:15–17).

For Jeshua, Zerubbabel, and Nehemiah, overcoming opposition always meant invoking a greater authority. No matter who the naysayers were, when these men appealed to the authority granted them by the different Persian kings, the opposition relented. God used the earthly authority of Persian kings to advance His work of rebuilding Jerusalem.

The fourth step in restoration is to deal with the sin in the land.

I am calling this the fourth step, but it happens throughout the restoration process. While the Temple, the wall, and the gates were being rebuilt, the leaders and the prophets were also dealing with the sin of the people.

At every point of restoration, sin is being addressed. It was not enough to rebuild the physical structures, the people's hearts needed to be cleansed. According to Ezra 9–10 and Nehemiah 13, the major sin issues of the people were intermarrying with non-Israelites, not tithing, and not observing the Sabbath and other holy days. The sin of intermarrying was so prevalent that Nehemiah responded violently:

> So I contended with them and cursed them and struck some of them and pulled out their hair, and made them swear by God, "You shall not give your daughters to their sons nor take their daughters for your sons or for yourselves. Did not Solomon king of Israel sin regarding these things?" (Nehemiah 13:25).

God intended the land to be pure, abundant, and life-giving. Getting there required dealing with the sin in the land.

God's work in Jerusalem happened as His people received and responded to His word. As He led, the people followed. Freedom came through obedience. But it did not come overnight. The fall of Jerusalem was a downward spiral that took over 300 years plus 70 years in captivity. Restoration was not going to be instantaneous.

But God was there, in the Temple, orchestrating His plan.

God is always working His plan.

Few people could foresee the fullness of what God was doing. Unfortunately, Jerusalem never returned to the glory it had during the reigns of David and Solomon. For the next 400 years the city would pass from world power to world power, eventually ending up in the hands of the Roman Empire.

However, what seemed like the languishing of a once great city was a part of God's plan to prepare a way for the coming of His Son, the Lord Jesus Christ, who would offer restoration and forgiveness to all people.

Conclusion

The city of Jerusalem can be a powerful metaphor for understanding who you are and how God works to free you. It is the will of God that His people be free. God built Jerusalem not to survive or make it through, but to shine. Each component of Jerusalem—its Temple, walls, gates, and land—were to be holy to the Lord.

If Israel would have listened and obeyed, the city would have endured as THE city. As you turn to look at your life, take with you what you have seen from the Lord and His work in Jerusalem.

ENEMIES

Before anything was created, God existed in spirit. God existed in perfection as Father, Son, and Holy Spirit. Each person of the Trinity was in complete love with the others. At some point, the Father determined to make angels, men, and creation so that they could enjoy life and love in the Trinity. In six days God made and filled the heavens and the earth. "God saw all that He had made, and behold, it was very good. And there was evening and there was morning, the sixth day" (Genesis 1:31).

Then there was a rebellion in the heavenlies. One of the lead angels, Lucifer, rebelled against God, jealous of His power and His position. (This event is alluded to in Isaiah 14:12–15 and Ezekiel 28:1–19.) Because of his rebellion, Lucifer was kicked out of the Divine Assembly. Lucifer was so cunning that he convinced a third of the angels to go with him. (See Revelation 12:3–4, where stars symbolize angels.) He became Satan and the fallen angels became demons. The war between the Kingdom of God and the kingdom of darkness began.

What started in the heavenlies came to earth when Satan took the form of a serpent and tempted Adam and Eve to rebel against God's commands. Adam and Eve fell, disobeying God. Because of their actions, sin entered the world, man surrendered control of the world to Satan, and, most tragically, man was separated from the God who loved and created him. Consequently, "We know that we are of God, and that the whole world lies in the power of the evil one" (1 John 5:19).

From the sin of Adam, man has been born into a world at war. All of the selfishness, disease, suffering, injustice, violence, wars, rebellion, and other forms of disobedience are a result of the war.

Who Are the Persons and Forces Binding You?

As in the days of Jerusalem, there are persons and forces actively working against your freedom in the Father, Son, and Holy Spirit. These persons and forces attack your city, i.e. your relationship with God, your identity, what you take in to yourself, and what you do. They lob bombs, shoot flaming arrows, attempt to sneak in, and operate in deceit and subtlety. The goal is the same: to steal, kill, and destroy you and your relationship with the Father, Son, and Holy Spirit. You need to know these sources so that you can get free and live free.

The three sources of bondage are sin, the world, and Satan. "And you were dead in your trespasses and sins, in which you formerly walked according to the course of this world, according to the prince of the power of the air, of the spirit that is now working in the sons of disobedience" (Ephesians 2:1–2). These three form an unholy trinity aggressively fighting to keep you from God's restoration. These are not nebulous or ambiguous forces. Each of these are intensely powerful and completely destructive. As we work through these you will be able to label the illustration of your own "city" with the correct source of your bondage.

Sin

Sin is rebellion against God and His will for your life. Sin is the killer. The world and Satan are both mainly external. (Certainly the demonic has the ability to enter into your life. However, that is not their "normal" place. On the contrary, your sin's native habitat is in you.) Sin lives in you. Sin fills your temples, tears downs your walls, laughs at your gates, and corrupts your land. So sinister and destructive is sin that the *only* solution is the sacrificial death of the Son of God.

Do not minimize or trifle with sin.

There are three types of sin that you battle:

Garden Sin

Man first fell in the Garden of Eden. Consequently, every person is born bearing the consequence and mark of Adam and Eve's original sin. It is important to understand that the mark of original sin is different for women than it is for men.

In Genesis 3:16, God curses Eve for her sin saying, "I will greatly multiply your pain in child birth, in pain you will bring forth children; Yet your desire will be for your husband, and he will rule over you." The mark of sin on the woman comes in her role as mother and wife. More than any other area of life, women will be confronted with insecurity in these two roles. Nothing she does as a mother ever makes her feel like she is doing enough. Every woman battles this. This is not coincidental. It is a mark of sin from Eve in the Garden of Eden.

Additionally, every woman struggles in their relationships with their spouses. When single, women struggle with an intense desire to be married. Then, when married, every woman wants to control their husbands.

These are not just "normal" patterns of behavior; they are the manifestations of original sin. Because of Eve's sin in the Garden, every woman bears these areas of sin: rebelling against God and His word for their lives as wives and mothers. This sin corrupts the identity of women and corrodes their land.

The curse for men is different. God curses Adam in Genesis 3:17–19, saying:

> Because you have listened to the voice of your wife, and have eaten from the tree about which I commanded you, saying, "You shall not eat from it"; Cursed is the ground because of you; In toil you will eat of it all the days of your life. Both thorns and thistles it shall grow for you; and you will eat the plants of the field; By the sweat of your face you will eat bread, till you return to the ground, because from it you were taken; For you are dust, and to dust you shall return.

Whereas woman is cursed as a mother and a wife, man is cursed as a provider. Man bears the consequence of sin as he battles every day to work and provide for his family. Because the ground is cursed, man receives a poor return for the effort he gives. Every man wars against insecurity in what he has. It is not coincidental that all men everywhere fight this fight. It is a manifestation of the curse of Adam's garden sin.

Men respond to Adam's sin by either increasing their work hours or by caving underneath the pressure. One man takes on additional projects and works 70–80 hours a week and effectively leaves his family in order to satisfy his role as provider. Another man can no longer handle the pressure and frustration of work and takes his life.

Neither honors the Lord.

Both are sin.

Both corrupt the land of man's life.

We are all born into garden sin. It is a powerful force in our lives leading us away from trusting God and His word for our lives, families, and provision.

As you consider the condition of your city, how is garden sin effecting your life? How prevalent of an issue is this in your life? When you diagram your city, label this as "OS" for Original Sin. Make the letters bigger or smaller depending on how much of a role Original Sin is playing in your bondage.

Generational Sin

Generational sins are those sin patterns passed down to us from our parents. Like garden sin, we are born in to our specific generational sin.

There is a really clear picture of this seen in the lineage of King David. David's dad was a man named Jesse. David was the eighth of Jesse's sons. By all accounts, Jesse lived a righteous life. There is certainly no indication at all that he had any sexual sin in his life. David, however, engaged in significant sexual sin. According to 2 Samuel 3:2–5 David had six children by six different women. 2 Samuel 5:13 says, "Meanwhile, David took more concubines and wives from Jerusalem, after he came from Hebron; and more sons and daughters were born to David."

Solomon, David's son, picked up his dad's sin. 1 Kings 11:3–4 says, "He had seven hundred wives, princesses, and three hundred concubines, and his wives turned his heart away. For when Solomon was old, his wives turned his heart away after other gods; and his heart was not wholly devoted to the Lord his God . . . ." In verses 5–8, Solomon added idolatry to his sexual sin. There were now graven images to foreign gods in the land of God's people.

Consequently, God tore ten tribes away from Solomon's son Rehoboam. Because of generational sin, Israel was now divided. Rehoboam and Abijam, Rehoboam's son and third generation from David, continued in the sex and idolatry of their fathers.

It was not until Asa, Abijam's son, became king that he sought to break the generational sin that affected him. 2 Kings 15:9–15 says that Asa removed all the idols from the land. Asa took a stand, drew a line, and dealt with most of his generational sin. Unfortunately, his forefathers passed on layers and layers of sin. Verse 14 says that even though the idols were removed, "The high places were not taken away; nevertheless, the heart of Asa was wholly devoted to the Lord all his days." While Asa did exceptional work in overturning generational sin, he did not get to all of it.

We also see generational sin as the reason God raised up Babylon to destroy Jerusalem. Jeremiah 16:10–13 says:

> Now when you tell this people all these words, they will say to you, "For what reason has the Lord declared all this great calamity against us? And what is our iniquity, or what is our sin which we have committed against the Lord our God?" Then you are to say to them, "It is because your forefathers have forsaken Me," declares the Lord, "and have followed other gods and served them and bowed down to them; but Me they have forsaken and have not kept My law. You too have done evil, even more than your forefathers; for behold, you are each one walking according to the stubbornness of his own evil heart, without listening to Me. So I will hurl you out of this land into the land which you have not known, neither you nor your fathers; and there you will serve other gods day and night, for I will grant you no favor."

Dealing with generational sin is not easy. We are all born into family lines wrought with sin that have not been addressed. Generational sin can take all forms: anger, laziness, gluttony, pride, fear, lust, idolatry. It will be helpful to draw your family tree back three to four generations. What do you see? What are the sin patterns specific to your family line? Is your family prone to divorce, lying, anxiety, depression, suicide, alcoholism, failure, negativity, pride, gluttony, or other sin patterns?

When you draw your city, use the initials 'GS' to label any Generational Sin. Make the letters bigger or smaller depending on the impact they are having. If you are unsure of the size of the impact, ask the Holy Spirit to show you the power of generational sin in your life. In addition to the sin of the garden, generational sin is a powerful source of bondage in our lives.

Personal Sin

In one sense, all sin is personal sin. *No matter how sin gets into us we are responsible for it.* When we act, it is we who are acting. Even though Rehoboam was born with garden sin and the generational sin of lust and idolatry, he was still responsible for what he did.

I am differentiating this category of personal sin to house those sins that cannot be attributed to the garden or to generations. These are those we do all on our own!

God gives us several lists of sin in Scripture, like Exodus 20:1–17, Proverbs 6:16–20, Matthew 5–7, Romans 1:26–32, and Galatians 5:19–21. These lists are compiled in **Appendix 1 – Sin**. As extensive as these are, they are not exhaustive.

There are a group of sins that seem to be more "popular" that most people need to be freed from:

- Perfectionism
- Money/materialism/jealousy
- Unforgiveness/anger
- Occult
- Sexuality in all forms, including body image, masturbation, pornography, homosexuality, etc.
- Drugs and alcohol
- Unbelief, rebellion: This takes the form of outright rejection of God and His will.
- Fear: fear of failure, rejection, loneliness, etc.
- Rebellion against parents
- Food: This can be gluttony, anorexia, or any unhealthy attitude toward food.

All of this is active rebellion against God and His way for our lives. Like garden sin and generational sin, personal sin separates us from intimacy with our Creator and corrodes our lives. These things are the natural products of life without the Lord. Without the presence of God in our lives, we live in perpetual search of satisfying our souls. We try everything apart from surrendering our lives to the pursuit of God.

There are three specific types of personal sin that merit further discussion: vows, sexual sin, and victimization.

Vows are agreements we enter into, usually with ourselves, that are unholy. What makes a vow unholy is the way the vow negates the faithfulness of God and/or His love. For example:

- A teenager is abruptly broken up with by the person they were dating. The heartbroken teen makes a vow: "I will never allow another person to do that to me again." The rest of his or her life is filled with relationships they intentionally sabotage. Their fear leads them away from trusting God's faithfulness.

- A person vows that they will never turn out like his or her father. They make the statement, "I will never turn out like him." That is an unholy vow. It is unholy because this person has taken control of the outcome of their lives instead of trusting God. Their fear of turning out like their father causes them to reject the faithfulness of their Heavenly Father.

- A woman vows, "I will never live in poverty." She has taken control of her life and cut off God's leading. She has said to the Lord, "I will follow you as long as you do not make me poor." God may never "make her poor," but her vow is keeping her from completely surrendering to God's will in her life.

- A young girl was forced to speak on stage when she was five. She did not want to do it. She was pushed on stage and cried through the entire performance. At five she vowed she would never let another person push her into doing something she did not want to do and she would never speak in front of people again.

Jesus teaches in Matthew 5:33–37 that you are not to make false vows or oaths. You are to let your yes be yes and your no be no. Jesus gives these direct words because He understands the binding force of vows. To say, "I will never trust another person," is to be bound by that and, consequently, to live according to it. Thankfully, the Holy Spirit knows every vow you have made. He will expertly reveal every one of these in time and give you the opportunity to break them.

The second category is sexual sin. Sexual sin is set apart from other personal sins. Paul writes in 1 Corinthians 6:18, "Flee immorality. Every other sin that a man commits is outside the body, but the immoral man sins against his own body." Sexual sins create strongholds that need to be addressed. As uncomfortable as these may be, addressing each sexual sin will be necessary to be freed.

The third type of personal sin is that which comes from being victimized. It is a horrible reality that many people suffer because of what others have done and are doing. Victimization is a powerful source of sin in our lives and one the enemy uses with great skill to keep us from the love and life of God.

There are three classic stories of victimization in Scripture. One is the account of Joseph and his brothers in Genesis 37–50. Because of Joseph's arrogance, his brothers sold him into slavery and faked his death to his father. While Joseph was certainly arrogant, he did not deserve the evil his brothers did. He suffered the sin of others.

The second account is the victimization of Tamar. Tamar's story is found in 2 Samuel 13. She was raped by her half-brother, Amnon. Compounding her pain, her father, King David, did not do anything about it.

The third account is the victimization of Jesus. He was crucified by a government and a religion that forced themselves upon Him. Not only did they kill Jesus, they brutally tortured Him in the process. There are many graphic accounts describing the horror He innocently suffered. Like Joseph, Jesus suffered the sin of others.

Like Joseph, Tamar, and Jesus, many of us are victimized. We are abandoned, abused, neglected, raped, and beaten. We suffer in silence. We suffer in every way possible experiencing unknown depths of darkness. Anger turns into bitterness and then callousness. Our lives can become defined by what we have experienced. Consequently, there is no way for the light and love of Jesus to come in and heal.

If you have been victimized, while you were not responsible for what has been done to you, you are responsible for how you handle it. Being abused is not sin, but holding on to anger and bitterness is. God can turn horrific tragedies and deep pain into amazing things if you let Him.

One of the great blessings of walking with Jesus is that He is **FAR MORE POWERFUL** than anything anyone has done, or will do, to us. This does not negate or minimize your suffering in the slightest bit. What it does do is put your suffering in perspective relative to the incomparable power of Jesus. Because He is seated at the right hand of the Father, you have hope. Because He sent the Holy Spirit, you have an opportunity for life that no one can take away. As we walk through healing, if you have suffered, you will see how the Holy Spirit can free you and begin to heal you.

In your city, label victimization with a "V." Again, make the letter bigger or smaller depending on the influence your victimization exercises. Where there have been multiple cases of victimization by different people, use more than one "V."

With respect to personal sins, label your city using "PS" to show the sins you have done. What are the sins you have committed? What are the sins you were involved in that you are still being accused of or battle? If you are unsure, ask the Holy Spirit to show you the unresolved sin issues you have in your life. Where personal sin has been significant, make the PS bigger.

We will see how the love and power of the Father, Son, and Holy Spirit can restore every area of life, even the deepest victimization, which has been corrupted by sin.

- Garden Sin – OS
- Generational Sin – GS
- Personal Sin – PS
- Victimization - V

The World

Now let's look at the various forces of the world that war against your freedom. While sin works in us, the forces of the world press down on us. The world is the actions, beliefs, and practices of others. In the category of sin we look at individuals. In the category of the world we look at collective man. The world is the institutions, systems, philosophies, religions, cultures, and practices of large groups of people. Every message of the world is a lie—every one of them. No matter what the lie is, the intent is to lead you away from some facet of the truth and teachings of Jesus. As you believe these lies you begin to act out in sin. Worldly lies are deadly and nefarious. You need to allow the Spirit to show you the various lies you are believing.

The following passages help us understand the world:

> Do not be conformed to this world, but be transformed by the renewing of your mind, so that you may prove what the will of God is, that which is good and acceptable and perfect (Romans 12:2).

> See to it that no one takes you captive though philosophy and empty deception, according to the tradition of men, according to the elementary principles of the world, rather than according to Christ (Colossians 2:8).

> For by these He has granted to us His precious and magnificent promises, so that by them you may become partakers of the divine nature, having escaped the corruption that is in the world by lust (2 Peter 1:4).
>
> Do not love the world nor the things in the world. If anyone loves the world, the love of the Father is not in him. For all that is in the world, the lust of the flesh and the lust of the eyes and the boastful pride of life, is not from the Father, but is from the world. The world is passing away, and also its lusts; but the one who does the will of God lives forever (1 John 2:15–17).

The messages of the world will be different based on culture, age, gender, ethnicity, and other factors. Some examples of worldly lies are:

- Morality: Life is about being a good, moral person.
- False Christian teachings: The prosperity gospel.
- Artist subculture: I must rebel to be creative.
- Homosexual subculture: God made me this way and He wants me to be happy.
- Materialism: Spirituality is intellectually weak. If it cannot be seen it is not real.
- False religions: Mormonism and Jehovah's Witnesses both deny that Jesus is God the Son.
- Latin definition of manliness: Machismo teaches men that they are to treat women poorly.
- Western definition of female beauty: Only extremely skinny women with the right curves are attractive.
- Western definition of success: Whoever has the most toys wins.
- Athletic subculture: I am god.
- Rugged individualism: Individuals can succeed on their own.

These are some examples of the variety of messages from the world.

Again, worldly messages will differ according to a variety of factors. However, all worldly messages are lies. They all deny the sufficiency of Jesus and His word for life. Any message, from any source, that denies Jesus and His way of life is not from God. That message is trying to enter in to your city to lead you away from resting in the love and freedom of the Father, Son, and Holy Spirit.

Where do you see worldly messages in your life? What are the philosophies or ways of life you were taught? Can you see how those are contrary to Jesus and His teaching? As you draw your city, place a "W" outside the walls and draw a line to the specific sin that the world has incited. Draw the "W" bigger or smaller as needed.

Satan

The final persons that war against your freedom are Satan and his demonic army. Jesus spent a lot of time in His life fighting against the demonic. The gospels are filled with story after story of Jesus being demonically tempted, dealing with demonically possessed people, and training His disciples to fight a spiritual war. Satan and his demonic army were real and powerful beings in the time of Jesus.

After Jesus ascended, His disciples carried on the fight of extending the Kingdom of God, rescuing people from the domain of darkness. Paul admonished the believers in Corinth and Ephesus to know the "schemes" of the evil one. Peter warned followers of Jesus, "Be of sober spirit, be on the alert, your adversary the devil prowls around like a roaring lion, seeking someone to devour" (1 Peter 5:8). James says in James 4:7, "Submit therefore to God. Resist the devil and he will flee from you." John taught believers in 1 John 5:19, "We know that we are of God and that the whole world lies in the power of the evil one." Almost every New Testament book includes significant teaching, warning, and training concerning Satan and his demonic army. We are foolish to dismiss or minimize his present-day effect on our lives.

Jesus and His disciples give us a spectrum of ways Satan works in our lives. In the extreme, Satan can possess a person. He, or one of his demons, can take a person over and control them. One place we see this form of Satan's work is in Luke 8:26–39. A demon-possessed man lived naked in a tomb. When he saw Jesus, he came running to Him. Jesus freed the man from his possession.

At the other end of the spectrum, Satan can tempt a person to sin. Satan sought to tempt Jesus to sin in Luke 4:1–13.

In the middle of temptation and possession are oppression and attachment. Oppression and attachment are different degrees of the same attack. Both are found in the same passages of Scripture. Paul writes in Ephesians 6:16, "In addition to all, taking up the shield of faith with which you will be able to extinguish all the flaming arrows of the evil one." The enemy is seen as one who is firing arrows at his targets. In our city metaphor, he is trying to lob arrows over the gates and walls of our lives.

Oppression happens when the enemy continues to lob the same dart at the same target. While he has not gained any ground, we feel continually under attack. Attachment happens when those arrows land again and again. Then they begin to spread. The enemy has penetrated our walls. We have given him access. This will feel like an unwinnable battle. No matter what a person does, they cannot get traction in this area of their lives. Where oppression can easily be thrown off by quoting Scripture, the same practice is ineffective in attachment. There is a deeper root involved that must be confronted.

It is important to understand that while followers of Jesus can be tempted, oppressed, and have demons attached to their lives, they cannot be possessed. Once a person gives their life to the Lord, the Holy Spirit enters in. The new believer is born again and unable to be possessed. This does not mean, however, that demons cannot do significantly debilitating damage to Christians. They can and they do. It simply means that a Christian cannot be taken over by a demon.

> **The spectrum of Satan's work in our lives:**
> - Temptation
> - Oppression
> - Attachment
> - Possession

We can see how the enemy works by looking at his names. His names reveal the kinds of thoughts, feelings, and experiences we are going to have when we are dealing with demonic issues. As you read through these, note how many of these are familiar to you in specific areas of your life.

Satan (Matthew 4:10, Job 1:6)
Satan means adversary. Satan works against God's will in people's lives. He may use fear, discouragement, distraction or a number of other weapons. Here he stands opposed to the direction of God for His people's lives.

Devil (Matthew 4:1, 13:39; Revelation 12:9)
Devil means slanderer or false accuser. Satan works to call people names, remind them of things past, and confuse them about the faithfulness of God.

Serpent (Genesis 3:1, 14; 2 Corinthians 11:3)
This name is used to highlight Satan's deceptive nature. He can take different forms and speak through different people. He does not just come straight forward or through one person.

Be-elzebul, Ruler of this world, Prince of the power of the air
(Matthew 10:25, 12:24; Luke 11:15, John 12:31, Ephesians 2:2)
Be-elzebul means lord of the house. All three have the same connotation. Satan is lord over the world. He exercises his authority from what Paul calls the air. We will see in the next section how Satan uses his authority, but it is important to understand he does have real authority.

Evil one (Matthew 13:19, 1 John 2:13)

It's pretty clear what this means, but here we pick up the nature of his intent. The being of Satan is evil. His works are evil. Evil is the enemy of God's goodness. Satan's intent is to bring desolation, destruction, and division.

Father of lies (John 8:44)

This is clear as well. He is the master liar. If he cannot get in with one lie, he will seek to get in with another. If neither works, he will lay in wait until an opportune time to return.

The Tempter (Genesis 3:1–3, Luke 4:1–13, Matthew 16:23)

Satan works through tempting. He lies, tempting people to question what they believe or never pursue truth at all. Notice that in the wilderness with Jesus Satan tried three different ways to tempt Jesus. Like lying, Satan tried to get in one way and it did not work, so he tried two others. When those failed he waited again until that opportune time.

Understanding these names will help you identify where Satan may be working in your life. The longer you fight in the war the more apparent Satan and his schemes will be. While he is a master liar, there's only so much he can do.

In addition to his names, we also see specific works Satan does in Scripture. These will further help us identify when he is the source of the issues with which we are dealing.

Today he is actively working by:

- Stealing the effectiveness of the Word in people's lives (Mark 4:15)
- Physical illness (Luke 13:10–17)
- Possession (Matthew 8:28, Mark 1:32, Luke 8:27)
- Blinding people in unbelief (2 Corinthians 2:11)
- False religions (John 8)
- Discord in the body of Christ (1 Corinthians 4:18–20)
- Extreme bodily harm (Luke 8:30)
- Subverting the will of God (Matthew 16:23)
- Keeping believers in bondage (James 4:7)

He is certainly doing more than this, but these are some key areas where he operates. (For an excellent study on the enemy's use of psychological warfare, see 2 Kings 18:13–19:37 and 2 Chronicles 32. Additionally, *The Strategy of Satan* by Warren Wiersbe is one of many great books on the subject.) If you identify these works in yourself, you need to discern the source and properly deal with it.

Do you believe you are under some form of demonic attack? Are the things you battle debilitating? Have you tried quoting Scripture and it hasn't worked? Do you have vivid images from your past continually "thrown" at you? Do you feel like the battle you're fighting is unwinnable?

As you draw your city, use the letter "D" to designate areas of sin that may be under demonic control. Draw a line from the "D" to the specific area(s) of sin involved. You may discern that the enemy is using a particular worldly lie to incite sin in a person. Draw a line from the "D" to the "W" to the correct label of sin in the person.

Sin, the world, and Satan are powerful forces working in our lives to keep us from the love of the Father, Son, and Holy Spirit. Understanding these will help you discern the various attacks you endure and will position you to walk in God's promised freedom.

Now let's consider how God has made you so that you can discern where attacks happen.

THE CITY OF YOU

Like the city of Jerusalem, God means our lives to be strong and powerful. He made us to be in relationship with Him as sons and daughters. "See how great a love the Father has bestowed on us, that we would be called children of God; and such we are" (1 John 3:1). We are to be love-filled, strong, powerful, humble, joyful people. "For God has not given us a spirit of timidity, but of power and love and discipline" (2 Timothy 1:7).

Unfortunately, most of us do not experience this. We wall off sections of our lives from Him. We are confused in our faith. We try to hang on to pieces of the world. We "negotiate" special considerations with the Father. Consequently, our temple, walls, gates, and land look like desolate cities or vacant towns.

While there are many versions of what our cities look like, three types are common. The first are those who have invited Jesus into their lives, but they do not let Jesus put His hands on certain areas of their lives. They have been deceived into believing they can successfully negotiate a way to have a relationship with God and hold onto areas of junk in their lives. Because it takes energy to manage issues kept from God and those issues hinder intimacy, these people are exhausted and empty.

The second group are those who have responded to life by allowing their walls to be torn down. They have no gates. Whatever goes, goes. They live useless lives because they feel useless. Nothing matters. Even though they do very little, they are still exhausted and empty.

The third group are those who have responded to life by hardening themselves. Their walls are thick. They build walls around their temples. They are distant people. These people can be friendly, but they're difficult to get close to. They tend to be highly disciplined and highly motivated. However, like the others, they are exhausted and empty.

Which one are you? How readily do you let God speak to every area in your life?

As you consider the "city of your life," how do you think it looks?

Getting free and staying free requires an honest, ongoing assessment of your life and your relationship with the Lord.

The good news is that no matter what your city looks like, God can restore, free, and empower you. Freedom and restoration are the heartbeat and will of God! "It is not those who are healthy who need a physician, but those who are sick . . . for I (Jesus) did not come to call the righteous, but sinners" (Matthew 9:12-13). He patiently waits to deliver you from everything that keeps you from experiencing the life He has for you.

We have exposed the persons and forces in the war. Now we are going to look at how God has made you. Then you will draw your city.

How God Has Made You

Temple
Like Jerusalem, you have been made with a temple. Your temple is the deepest, most central part of who you are. It is the place in you that defines you. It is the source from which everything else flows. It is the place of deepest peace, deepest power, and deepest longing. In your personal temple there is an outer court, a holy place, and a holy of holies. Many people are allowed in your outer courts. A select few gain access to the holy place. But no one can get into your holy of holies except God Himself. Your holy of holies has been designed to be filled by one person and one person only: God. There is nothing in all of creation, visible or invisible, thought or emotion, that can satisfy this place but God. No one else can get in. No one.

An empty or unhealthy holy of holies will cause deep instability. This makes sense because your holy of holies is "below" everything else in you. Your biology, chemistry, personality, dreams, desires, accomplishments, and everything else are above your temple. So, even though you experience success in some or all of these areas, you're still hounded by instability, insecurity, fear, and dissatisfaction.

We see this clearly with Adam and Eve. God made them to be in fellowship with Him. There was no sin in their land. They were filled with God's presence and walked in His ways. God commanded them that they could eat out of any tree of the Garden of Eden except the Tree of the Knowledge of Good and Evil. God warned them that if they ate from that tree they would die.

Giving into demonic temptation, Adam and Eve ate from the tree and died. Now, they did not physically die. But that was not the death about which God warned. There is a greater death than physical death. The death God warned them of was relational death. When Adam and Eve ate from the tree, their intended relationship with God died. They immediately changed from a place of intimacy and fullness with God to a place of separation and emptiness.

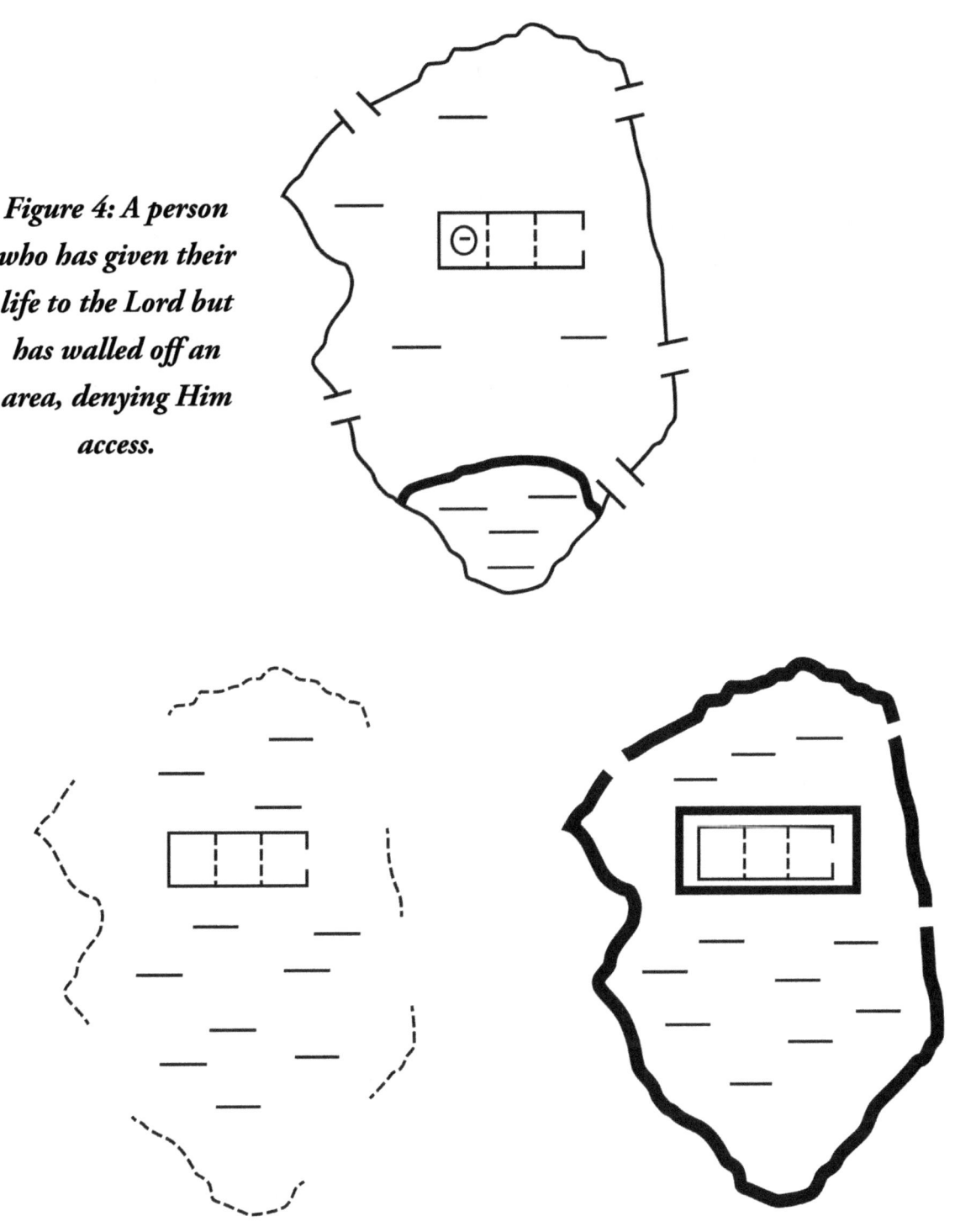

Figure 4: A person who has given their life to the Lord but has walled off an area, denying Him access.

Figure 5: A person who has responded to life by allowing their walls to be torn down. Gates are almost nonexistent.

Figure 6: A person who has responded to life by hardening their walls. Gates are almost nonexistent.

Genesis 3:7–10 records Adam and Eve's experience after eating from the tree:

> Then the eyes of both of them were opened, and they knew that they were naked; and they sewed fig leaves together and made themselves loin coverings. They heard the sound of the Lord God walking in the garden in the cool of the day, and the man and his wife hid themselves from the presence of the Lord God among the trees of the garden. Then the Lord God called to the man, and said to him, "Where are you?" He said, "I heard the sound of You in the garden, and I was afraid because I was naked; so I hid myself."

Because of their separation, Adam and Eve experienced shame, guilt, and fear. Where they could walk in innocence, freedom, and joy, they now lived in hiding, seeking to cover what they had done.

Their emptiness caused their instability.

When any person surrenders their life to the Lord, He comes into their holy of holies, His place in them. Jesus says in John 15:5:

> I am the Vine, you are the branches; He who abides in Me and I **in him**, he bears much fruit, for apart from Me you can do nothing (emphasis added).

There is a place in you where Jesus can abide that before He came in was not occupied. The place where Jesus abides in you is the temple.

Paul writes in Galatians 4:4-7:

> But when the fullness of the time came, God sent forth His Son, born of a woman, born under the Law, so that He might redeem those who were under the Law, that we might receive the adoption as sons. Because you are sons, God has sent forth the Spirit of His Son into our hearts, crying, "Abba! Father!" Therefore you are no longer a slave, but a son; and if a son, then an heir through God.

There is much discussion about what Paul means by the word "heart." I understand his use of the word in this verse to mean the deepest part of a person. It is equivalent to our temple.

Whenever a person gives their life to Jesus, God the Father sends the Holy Spirit into the life of that person. The deepest part of that person, once vacant and dark, is now filled and full of light. That person is immediately restored into relationship with God.

Oftentimes, restoration will require a person to deal with one or two major issues that are "blocking" God's entrance into their temple. These are issues keeping God from being number one in that person's life. One example of such a person is the rich, young ruler. His story is found in Luke 18:18-27:

> A ruler questioned Him, saying, "Good Teacher, what shall I do to inherit eternal life?" And Jesus said to him, "Why do you call Me good? No one is good except God alone. You know the commandments, 'Do not commit adultery, Do not murder, Do not steal, Do not bear false witness, Honor your father and mother.'" And he said, "All these things I have kept from my youth." When Jesus heard this, He said to him, "One thing you still lack; sell all that you possess and distribute it to the poor, and you shall have treasure in heaven; and come, follow Me."
>
> But when he had heard these things, he became very sad, for he was extremely rich. And Jesus looked at him and said, "How hard it is for those who are wealthy to enter the kingdom of God! For it is easier for a camel to go through the eye of a needle than for a rich man to enter the kingdom of God." They who heard it said, "Then who can be saved?" But He said, "The things that are impossible with people are possible with God."

Notice that this man had many, many things going for him. He was rich, young, powerful, and moral. What a life! However, in spite of everything he had going for him, he knew something was not right. He knew there was more.

Although he could not identify it, we know he was experiencing the emptiness of his temple. Everything he had—his wealth, age, power, and morality—sat above his temple. Because his temple was empty, nothing else was right.

So he sought out an answer from Jesus. Maybe he should be somewhat commended for seeking an answer at all. Too many people walk numb to the reality of their own discontent. Others walk in acceptance of theirs—this is just the way it is. This man felt his emptiness and wanted an answer. So he sought out Jesus.

Jesus told him he needed to sell all that he had and give it to the poor. If he would do that, then he would be filled and then he could follow Jesus. Famously, the man walks away grieved because he was extremely rich. (The story of the ruler obviously has to do with material wealth; however, I have found this same experience to be true with anyone who is rich in any area of their lives.) His love of money stood at the doorway to his temple and kept God from entering. It is normal for people to have one or two major issues keeping them from accepting the love of God. Are there specific issues in your life keeping you from giving your life to Jesus that need to be dealt with? What are they? As you work on drawing your city, put these issues in front of the door to your temple.

Toward the end of His earthly ministry Jesus spent concentrated time with His disciples. One of the topics He emphasized was the intimate nature of the relationship the Father, Son, and Holy Spirit was inviting them to embrace. Jesus wanted His disciples to understand the depth of the relationship. In John 14:16–17, Jesus says,

> I will ask the Father, and He will give you another Helper, that He may be with you forever; that is the Spirit of truth, whom the world cannot receive, because it does not see Him or know Him, but you know Him because He abides with you and will be in you.

In the same conversation Jesus continued, "If anyone loves Me, he will keep My word; and My Father will love him, and We will come to him and make Our abode with him" (John 14:23). The Father, Son, and Holy Spirit come into a person's life in the deepest place of their being.

Notice in these two passages that anyone who gives their life to Jesus comes into an equal relationship with all three persons of the Trinity. To be right with God is to be in right relationship with the Father, Son, and Holy Spirit. This is called living in Trinitarian balance. The Holy Spirit comes into the temple of the one who surrenders their life to God. The Holy Spirit can come in because Jesus, the Son, rose from the dead, overcoming sin, the world, and Satan according to the will of the Father. The Spirit carries out the will of the Father adopting the new believer into the family as a son or daughter of God.

Most people live in some form of Trinitarian imbalance. This occurs when a person is closer with one or two persons of the Trinity to the limiting or ignoring of the other(s). For example, a person feels close with the Spirit but rarely talks to or considers the Father. Or, a person relates easily with Jesus but has no contact with the Spirit. Trinitarian imbalance can take on different forms. Nevertheless, to have a strong, healthy temple, a person needs to be at rest in the love of the Father, Son, and the Holy Spirit.

Your temple is the place in you where you relate to the Father, Son, and Holy Spirit.

Walls

Your walls define who you are. They give you your identity. How you see yourself is very important to the Lord and a place of great vulnerability. The Apostle Paul begins his letter to the Colossians, "Paul, an apostle of Jesus Christ by the will of God, and Timothy our brother. To the saints and faithful brethren in Christ who are at Colossae; Grace to you and peace from God our Father." Paul identifies himself according to his relationship with Jesus. He is an apostle. Then he calls the Christians in Colossae, "saints and faithful brethren." These are the names God called each believer in Colossae. Whoever they were before they came to faith in Christ has died. Now, in Christ, they have new names.

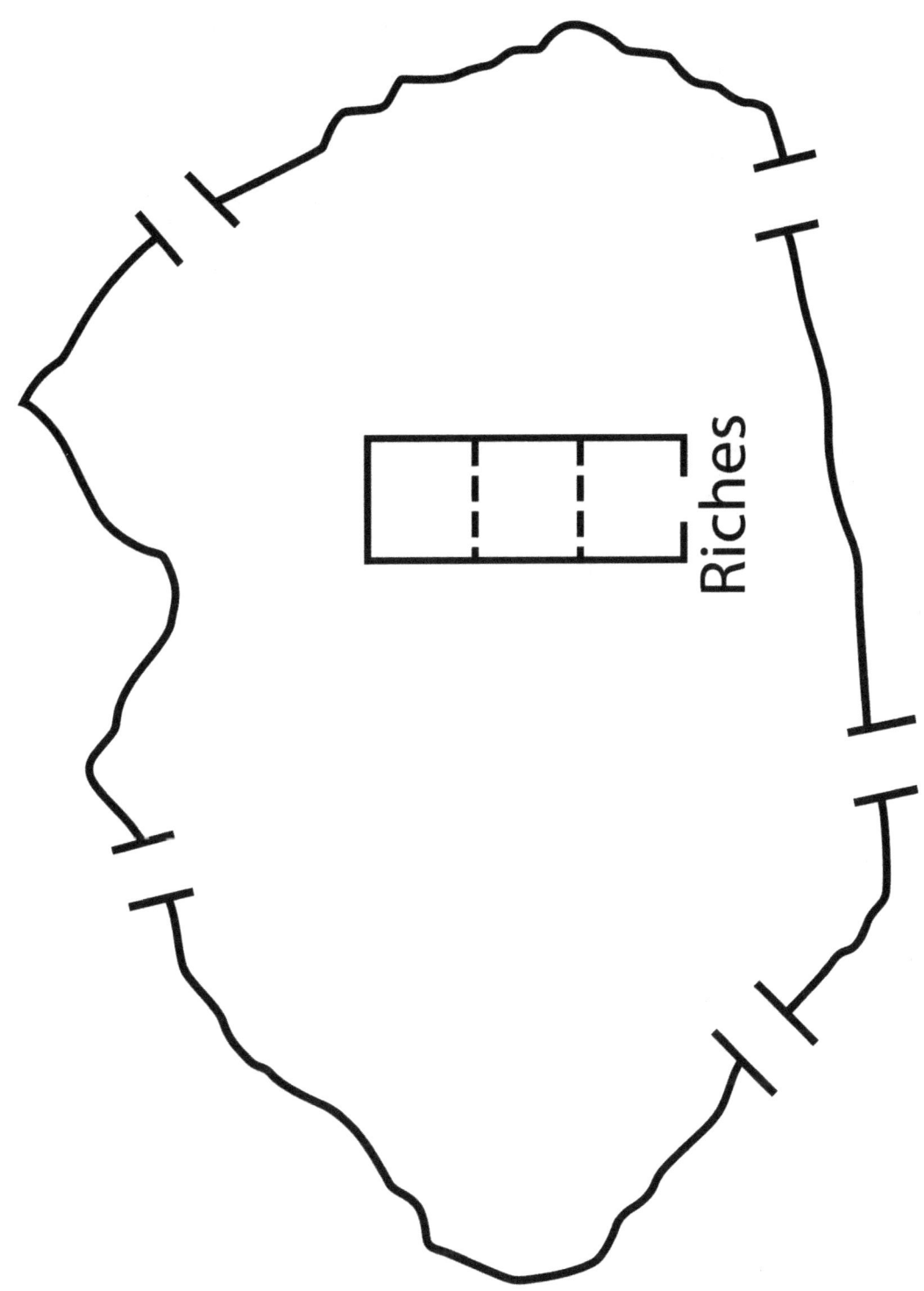

Figure 7: A picture of a person with riches blocking the entrance to their temple. Unless riches are dealt with, God cannot get in

Peter emphasizes his disciples' new names as well. He writes in 1 Peter 2:9, "But you are a chosen race, a royal priesthood, a holy nation, a people for God's own possession . . .." Peter, whose name was changed by Jesus from Cephas to Peter, knew the importance of his disciples embracing their new identity.

Furthermore, Jesus lived with a strong belief in who He was according to His relationship with His Father. Eight times in the book of John Jesus introduces His identity with the divine, "I AM." He says:

- "I am the bread of life" (John 6:35).
- "I am the light of the world"(John 8:12).
- "Before Abraham was, I am" (John 8:58).
- "I am the door" (John 10:9).
- "I am the good shepherd" (John 10:11).
- "I am the resurrection and the life" (John 11:25).
- "I am the way, the truth, and the life" (John 14:6).
- "I am the true vine" (John 15:1).

These names, and many others, were branded on the walls of Jesus's life. This is who He was every moment of every day of His life. These names anchored His identity. They provided an awareness of who He was and a defense against accusations that He was someone else.

It is important to remember that when you came to faith in Jesus, who you were before is gone. Your old identity has been crucified. Paul says in Galatians 2:20, "I have been crucified with Christ; and it is no longer I who live, but Christ lives in me; and the life which I now live in the flesh I live by faith in the Son of God, who loved me and gave Himself up for me." There are no exceptions to this. Everyone who comes to faith in Christ must first die to who they were.

In the healing process, you may need to identify who you were. Many times we remain in bondage in our identities because we have not fully accepted who we were. Jesus does not want you to ignore or minimize who you were. He wants you to confess the fullness of it to Him so that you can be fully forgiven and fully embrace your new life.

So, who were you? What were the names you were called? What were the names you lived by—good, bad, or both? What are the names you call yourself? What were the names you were indirectly called? A child whose father is nonexistent is never verbally called "worthless." Nevertheless, they take on that name because that is how their father made them feel.

Here are some examples of lies we can believe that corrupt our identity:

- *A lie from the world* – You believe you are ugly and undesirable because you do not fit the world's definition of beauty. Did you learn this lie from a specific magazine, television show, song, or person(s)?

- *A lie from a generational sin* – You are in a line of people who are alcoholics. They are alcoholics because they have taken on the name "failure." As you look in your family tree, there are failures everywhere.

- *A lie from personal sin* – You were wildly successful in athletics. You have more honors, awards, and trophies than you have room. You embraced the identity of "All-Star." While there have been many who have "pumped you up," you know that you are primarily responsible for taking on that identity.

- *A lie from victimization* – It was your uncle first. Later it was a cousin. The abuse was constant and lasted for years. No one knew. Because of what they did you took on the name "worthless whore."

- *A lie from the demonic* – You are accused day and night of everything possible so that you live in guilt and shame. No matter how hard you try, how much Bible you read, how many passages you memorize, how much counseling you go to, you cannot get out from underneath these accusations.

Your Heavenly Father is passionate about the names you have on your walls. The Scriptures are full of names God has for you. (See **Appendix 2 - Names God Calls Me** for a list.) With God in your temple, He wants you to declare on your walls:

"I am (your name), a Child of God!"

Branded on the walls of a follower of Jesus will be the names God calls you: "Chosen," "Son," "Daughter," "Righteous," and other truths about you. Your wall is who you are in light of His presence in you.

The names God calls you give you an awareness of who you are and a defense against accusations that you are anyone else.

Gates

Your gates control what gets in to and what comes out of your city. You have eight gates in your life: sight, smell, taste, touch, hearing, spirit, mind, and emotions. The things you watch on TV, read in the news and books, teachings you listen to, messages you were raised on, thoughts and feelings you consider, certain smells, and even the food you eat all enter into your city. They all affect the condition of your life.

Peter trains his disciples to have strong gates: "Fix your hope completely on the grace to be brought to you at the revelation of Jesus Christ" (1 Peter 1:13). Jesus lived with His gates focused on His Father: "Therefore Jesus answered and was saying to them, 'Truly, truly, I say to you, the Son can do nothing of Himself, unless it is something He sees the Father doing; for whatever the Father does, these things the Son also does in like manner'" (John 5:19). Your gates control what you set your senses on, what you allow in your city, and what comes out of your city.

Deuteronomy 6:4–9 gives us a real vivid picture of what God wants for our gates:

> Hear, O Israel! The Lord is our God, the Lord is one! You shall love the Lord your God with all your heart and with all your soul and with all your might. These words, which I am commanding you today, shall be on your heart. You shall teach them diligently to your sons and shall talk of them when you sit in your house and when you walk by the way and when you lie down and when you rise up. You shall bind them as a sign on your hand and they shall be as frontals on your forehead. You shall write them on the doorposts of your house and on your gates.

The word of God is supposed to be on the heart, forehead, hands, living room, bed room, doorposts, and gates! The word of God becomes a filter for understanding life and the Lord. Nothing gets in except the eternal, strong, pure, life-giving breath of the words of God. Those are ***powerful*** gates!

In Christ, God trains us to be pro-active in our thoughts and emotions. We learn to actively fill our minds with truth. We learn how to discipline our thoughts. Paul writes, "We are taking every thought captive to the obedience of Christ" (2 Corinthians 10:5). Our emotions are surrendered to the Holy Spirit so that His fruit can come out of us. "But the fruit of the Spirit is love, joy, peace, patience, kindness, goodness, faithfulness, gentleness, self-control; against such things there is no law" (Galatians 5:22–23). As followers of Jesus we are not pushed around by every puff of wind, in part because our gates are powerful filters. We reject every emotion, thought, and spirit that is not from the Lord. And we meditate daily on the glory, wonder, love, faithfulness, power, might, and joy of the Almighty God.

Land

In addition to a temple, walls, and gates, you also have land. Your land contains the sins you have committed, the pain you have suffered, and the dreams you have. Whereas your walls define who you are, your land is what you have done and what has been done to you. Paul writes in Colossians 3:8–10, "But now you also put them all aside: anger, wrath, malice, slander, and abusive speech from your mouth. Do not lie to one another, since you laid aside the old self with its evil practices, and have put on the new self . . . ." Anger, wrath, etc. are those things that were in the land of the Colossian people.

Jesus speaks to the sin in peoples' land in Matthew 5:21–48. In this section of His Sermon on the Mount, Jesus confronts sins of anger and unforgiveness, adultery, divorce, dishonesty, revenge, and judgmentalism. These are all sins in the land of the people He is speaking to.

God intends the land of His people to be holy. It is important to understand that all sin in your land is negative. You are a finite person who has limited space. Sin in your land takes space that cannot be filled with love or joy or peace or power. The great things of the Lord cannot move in until the trash of sin is taken out. No matter how far down a person tries to bury their trash, it is still in them. The odor pushes through the layers of ground causing all sorts of issues.

Peter writes in 1 Peter 1:14–15, "As obedient children, do not be conformed to the former lusts which were yours in your ignorance, but like the Holy One who called you, be holy yourselves also in all your behavior." This is God's desire because He is holy. And this is God's desire because our holiness, our cleansed and purified ground, will be filled with His glorious presence and all His promises.

It is possible for sin to be layered in your land. For example, alcoholism can sit on top of anger that can sit on top of rejection. Fear can produce anxiety that can lead to excessive working. Rejection can lead to overeating that can lead to a pornography problem. James 4:1–10 says that relational conflict can come from selfishness that is rooted in not trusting the Father. In dealing with sin in the land, we want to get to the root issues within. Thankfully, and mercifully, the Holy Spirit will always help to make known root issues.

Furthermore, sin can have multiple sources. Anxiety can come from a worldly lie of having to attain a certain level of material possessions to be successful, a generational sin, or original sin. Anger can be demonic and personal. Gluttony can come from a worldly lie and from victimization. It is normal for there to be more than one source for an area of sin. Regardless of how many sources there are to sin, God wants to expose all the causes and deal with them.

Your land holds the consequences of disobeying God's will. It holds lies you have believed. The wounds and weariness of your rebellion are kept in your land. Your land also holds what you want to do—your hopes, dreams, and desires. Your past, present, and future are held here.

---

4 Components of Your City:
- Temple = Relationship with God
- Walls = Who we are
- Gates = What gets in
- Land = What we do

Cities of Others

We have covered the war you live in and how God has made you. We're going to walk through three examples of others' cities so that you can continue to see how these persons and forces work. The first example is a conglomeration of people with whom I have worked. The second and third examples are two people I have known.

The first generic example is of a person who has given their life to Jesus but has multiple, unresolved issues stemming from multiple sources. Through this example you can see the different possibilities such issues present.

Sources of Bondage

1. Sin:
   - OS: Original Sin
   - GS: Generational Sin
   - PS: Personal Sin
   - V: Victimization
2. W: World
3. D: Satanic/Demonic

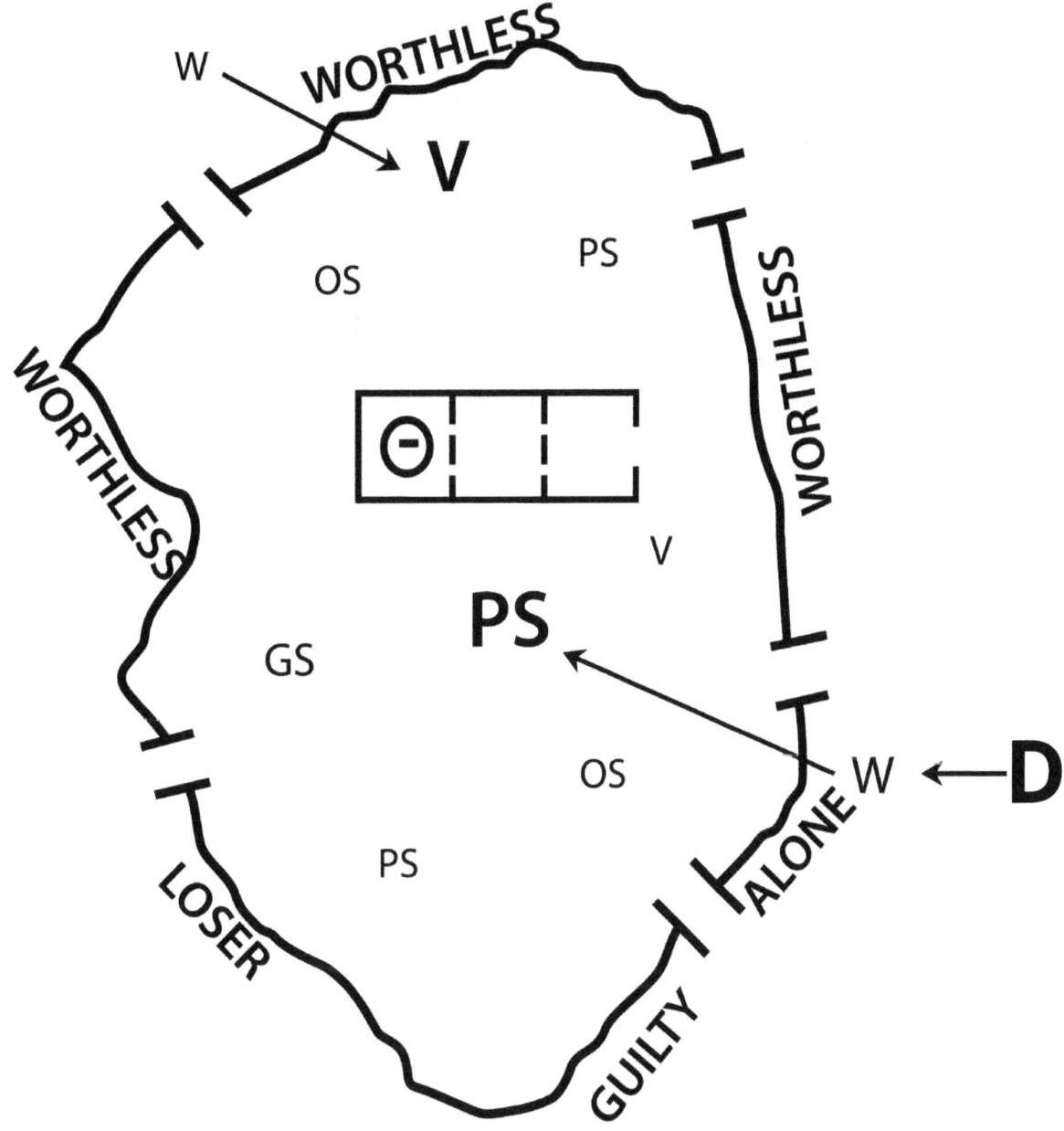

Figure 8: A person who has accepted Christ but has many unresolved issues keeping them in bondage.

A second example is a man named Bill. (All names have been changed to protect the confidentiality of those mentioned, but all of their stories are being used with their permission.)

Bill had known the Lord for ten years. He serves in his church and on the board of a Christian ministry, and he actively supports missionaries. In the past four years, he started to suffer debilitating panic attacks to the point that he could not drive his children to their events. When we met, I heard the rest of his story.

I discovered that Bill's anxiety ultimately comes from his unwillingness to trust God as his Father. He was suffering from a combination of original, generational, and personal sin.

The original sin was obvious: the effect of Adam strikes men in the place of provider and protector. The worldly lie came through separate experiences with his mom and dad. His mom had continually told him, "You can do anything you set your mind to." But his dad had led a chaotic life, constantly moving the family and chasing a dream he never caught. He lived in financial anxiety.

Bill responded to his mom by believing that he truly could do anything. He responded to his dad by determining that he would never live the way his dad did. While that may sound good, his life was motivated by fear, not by faith. Through the lie, a demonic spirit attached himself to Bill's life and overwhelmed him. He was so unaware of the lie that for the duration of his time in the Lord he always prayed to Jesus and never to the Father.

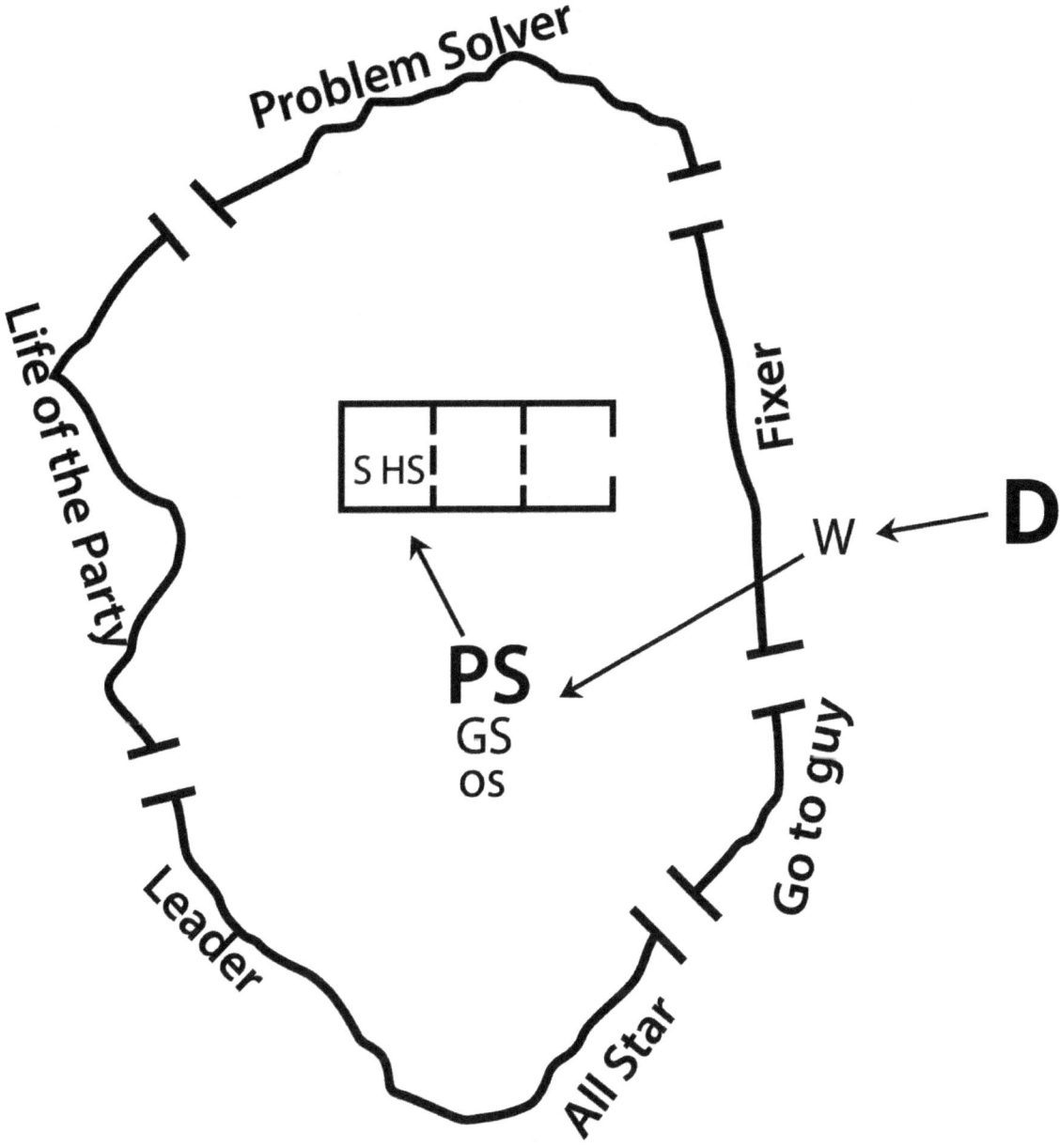

Figure 9: Bill's city showing his demonic attachment that produced Trinitarian imbalance.

The third example is a woman named Melinda. Melinda wanted nothing to do with the Lord. She grew up in church but rebelled against her parents, leaving home when she was sixteen. We met when she was twenty four.

Over a series of meetings, it came out that she had a strong fear of being turned into just another hypocritical religious person. While there was no direct demonic attachment, the enemy was using images Melinda had seen and experiences she'd had with hypocritical Christians in the past to keep her from the love of the Father, Son, and Holy Spirit. The door to Melinda's heart had been *barricaded* by religion.

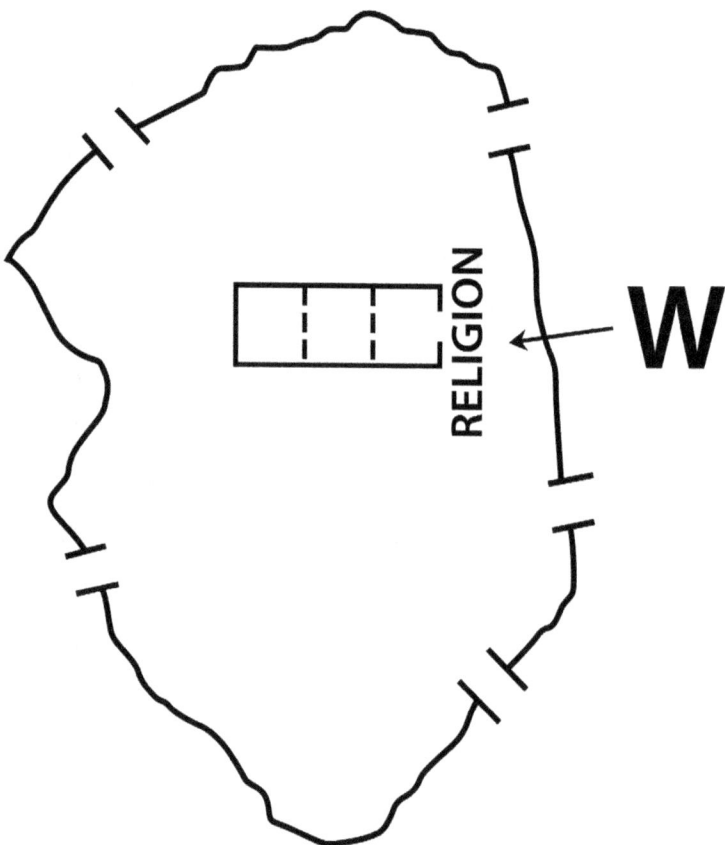

Figure 10: Melinda's city showing the effect of a worldly lie.

Both Bill and Melinda were freed from the issues binding them. Both have continued to live freely and grow in maturity, and are being used powerfully in the Kingdom. All three of these examples should help you continually sharpen your view of your own city.

Draw Your City

Now it's time to draw. What is the condition of your city? Walk through each section and observe what you see. After you observe what you see, ask the Holy Spirit to show you what He sees. Listen well. Draw your city.

Temple – How is your relationship with God?

- Are there major issues in your life keeping you from surrendering your life to Him?
- Do you walk in intimacy with each person of the Trinity? Is there a person of the Trinity you are closer with than the others?
- Are you angry with God because of something you perceive He did or did not do?
- What are the sources of the separation you have in your relationship?

Walls – What is your identity?

- What are the names you were called growing up either directly or indirectly?
- Who called you these names?
- Are there other sources that have compounded these names in your life?
- What are the objects you have that remind you of these names?

Gates – What are your inputs?

- What do you take in that is not of the Lord? (TV shows, news, entertainment, teachings, etc.)
- Do you dwell on negative images or memories?
- Are you passive or active, or pro-active or reactive, in your thoughts and emotions?

Land – How do you actively engage in sin? What are the things that have been done to you that are unresolved?

- How does original sin affect you?
- What is the generational sin, if any, that you see in your family line?
- How have you been victimized? By whom? How are you dealing with it?
- What are the things people have done to you that you are still carrying? Whom do you need to forgive?
- What are the things you have pursued because of worldly lies you have believed?
- What are the dominant areas of personal sin where you are guilty?
- If sexual sin is in your land, you will need to write down the names of those you have been with sexually. No matter how short or long the list is, you need to write them down. If you do not remember every name, then have a final category called "others."

How does your city look? Quite a mess?! Do not fear or be ashamed. God has known this for a very long time. This is why Jesus died! He did not die because you scraped your knee. He died because we are all wholly and completely messed up! He died to break the power of sin, the world, and Satan so that freedom could be made available to all.

Take your city and convert it to the **Freedom Worksheet** found in **Appendix 3**. The Freedom Worksheet simply lists what your city shows. You will be set free as you work through what you have on your list. Where you need more space, use additional paper.

In the final chapter, you will learn how to get free.

FREEDOM

Everything in freedom has to do with power. Everything. Bondage is all about being held by someone or something that has more power than you have. You have lived your life feeling like there was nothing you could do. You've felt powerless. The best you have been able to do is manage what you battle. Victory? Not happening.

Everything in freedom has to do with power.

The Good News is that when Jesus ascended into heaven He was raised "far above all rule and authority and power and dominion" (Ephesians 1:21). He overcame sin, the world, and Satan and was eternally seated at His Father's right hand. Consequently, there is no power in heaven or on earth that is greater than Him. And it is not even close!

When a person gives their life to Jesus, the Holy Spirit comes, equipping them with the same power and authority Jesus had! Jesus said in John 14:12, "Truly, truly, I say to you, he who believes in Me, the works that I do, he will do also; and greater works than these he will do; because I go to the Father." Paul wrote in Ephesians 1:18, "I pray that the eyes of your heart may be enlightened, so that you will know . . . *what is the surpassing greatness of His power toward us who believe*" (emphasis added). In fact, Paul writes in 1 Corinthians 2:1–5 that his preaching came in the power of God, "so that your faith would not rest on the wisdom of men, but on the power of God." Your faith is supposed to depend upon the power of God!

Because of our Father's love for us, Jesus came in the power of the Holy Spirit to conquer His, and our, enemies. It is crucial that you believe and walk in the power and authority of Jesus that is poured out on us by the Holy Spirit according to the will of the Father. Your freedom is a work of the Trinity! It is the will of our Father that you be freed from bondage. Jesus is the person of the Trinity who came, defeated sin, the world, and Satan, and was raised far above all powers to sit at the Father's right hand. The Holy Spirit brings with Him the power of Jesus when we surrender our lives. If you are not familiar with walking in the power of Jesus, you need to learn so that you can be effective in walking in freedom and helping others.

Being freed is a **power confrontation** between Jesus and whatever or whoever is the source of bondage. There is a literal clash as Jesus is unleashed through the Spirit against His enemies. He will win—that was settled. He always wins. Living freely happens as we rest in the power of Jesus and exercise it against His enemies who continually assail us.

You should know and feel Triune power and authority when you're dealing with freedom issues. If you don't know Triune power, then you need to learn. The Father, Son, and Holy Spirit work together to set us free because they can!

As you go through your healing, use the **Freedom Worksheet** as it will help you get through each area.

Temple: Healing Our Relationship with Him

God restores your temple as you turn to Him and deal seriously and honestly with the condition of your relationship with the Father, Son, and Holy Spirit. In each area of need you will confess your sin and repent, renounce the source and reject its hold over you, and embrace the forgiveness and truth of your Father. Confess, repent, renounce, reject, and embrace are the five steps we will work through in each area of our lives.

- If you have one or two dominant issues blocking the door to your temple and you are ready to get healed, then confess each area:

    "Father, in the name of Jesus, I confess to You that I have rejected You and held on to my riches. I repent of this sin, Father. I renounce the worldly lie that riches are life and reject the authority and control this lie has exercised in me. I embrace your truth that life is in Jesus! I declare that You are my God! I lay my riches down to you and will faithfully follow whatever you have for me to do."

    As you are working through the Freedom Worksheet, mark a line through this issue. It no longer controls you.

- If you walk in Trinitarian imbalance you need to confess that to whichever person(s) of the Trinity you have neglected:

    "Holy Spirit, in the name of Jesus, I confess I have not sought intimacy with You. I repent of the lies of my denomination and the materialistic culture I was taught. I renounce the lies and reject the authority they have exercised over me. I embrace You! I embrace Your forgiveness!"

    Mark a line through this issue. It no longer controls you.

- If you have been angry at any one of the Father, Son, or Holy Spirit because of what you perceived they did or did not do, then you need to take responsibility for your sin:

"Father, I confess I am angry at You. You did not stop my mother from getting sick, dying, and leaving me. Why didn't you heal her? I confess I have been very angry at You. I understand now that this is sin. I repent of this sin. I renounce the lie that You are not good, faithful, and wise. I reject the demonic that have been attacking me in this area. I command you, in the name of Jesus, to leave me. The Bible says, 'Submit therefore to God, resist the devil, and he will flee from you.' I have submitted this lie to God. You must flee from me. I reject you and your lie in the name of Jesus. Father, I declare that You are good, faithful, and wise. I embrace You and Your forgiveness."

It is certainly appropriate in a case like this that you ask the Father to show you whatever you need to see about His role in your mother's life so that you can have whatever clarity He wants you to have. Ask Him to show you.

Mark a line through this issue. It no longer controls you.

Pray through whatever other areas of sin and woundedness you have in your temple. Ask the Holy Spirit to show you anything else He wants to address.

After praying through these, receive this prayer from me on your behalf:

"Father, in the name of Jesus, this person has confessed and repented of their sin. According to Your word, 'If we confess our sins, He is faithful and righteous to forgive us our sins and to cleanse us from all unrighteousness' (1 John 1:9). Based on Your word, I declare this person is forgiven. To you I say, "In the name of Jesus, you are forgiven of this. Walk in your freedom!"

After restoring our temples, God will move to whatever area in us He wants to heal next. The walls and gates of Jerusalem were rebuilt at the same time sin was being dealt with in the land. In your healing it is important to let the Holy Spirit lead you to the places He wants to address. We will present ways the Spirit heals in different areas, but there is no order to these.

Walls: Healing Our Identity
God moves to heal your identity by dealing with the lies you have believed about yourself and the sources of those lies. Where you have believed these lies because of things people have said to you or made you feel, you will need to renounce the name and forgive them. Remember, Jesus has more

power than what has been done to you. You will always need the power of Jesus to forgive anyone. His power and His presence are available for you now. Where you have believed a lie because of a worldly or demonic lie, you will need to renounce the name and reject their authority.

- If you have taken on names people have called you directly or indirectly, with every name you have on your list, you need to pray this, or something similar to it:

"Father, in the name of Jesus, I confess that I was worthless. I believed that about myself. Right now I choose to renounce this name. I am no longer that person. Father, I choose to forgive _____ for every time they called me stupid. Father, you know how that made me feel and the damage it has done to me. In the name of Jesus—NO MORE. I am no longer that person! I renounce that name and reject the authority that I have given that name over me. I embrace You and who You say I am. You say that I am a 'temple of the Holy Spirit' filled with love, power, and life."

Now, mark a line through that name and that person(s) and move on to the next one.

- If you have taken on names from the world or from the demonic, with each name pray this:

"Father, in the name of Jesus, I confess that I have believed the lie that I am _____. I confess that I have believed what the world (or the enemy) has said about me more than what you say about me. I ask You to forgive me of this. I renounce this name. I am no longer _____ and declare that I am Your son/daughter. I reject this worldly lie (or the enemy). In the name of Jesus I break all authority and control that this name has had over me. I embrace You and who You say I am!"

Now, mark a line through that name and that source and move on to the next one.

- If you have taken on names from vows you have made, with each name pray this:

"Father, in the name of Jesus, I confess that I made a vow that _____. This is not of You. I ask You to forgive me of this. I renounce this vow and break the authority and control it has had in my life. I embrace Your love, faithfulness, and identity in my life."

Now, make a line through that name and move on to the next one.

Our identities are wrapped up in more than just the names we've been called. They can also be enforced by objects we have. Music, memorabilia, pictures, articles, and other things that are strong reminders of who we were may have strong power in our lives today. They need to be addressed.

Before the Apostle Paul surrendered his life to Jesus, he was advancing in Judaism beyond his contemporaries. Read how he deals with the things in his life that reminded him of who he was:

> If anyone else has a mind to put confidence in the flesh, I far more: circumcised the eighth day, of the nation of Israel, of the tribe of Benjamin, a Hebrew of Hebrews; as to the Law, a Pharisee; as to zeal, a persecutor of the church; as to the righteousness which is in the Law, found blameless. But whatever things were gain to me, those things I have counted as loss for the sake of Christ. More than that, I count all things to be loss in view of the surpassing value of knowing Christ Jesus my Lord, for whom I have suffered the loss of all things, and count them but rubbish so that I may gain Christ . . . (Philippians 4:4–8).

The word "rubbish" in the Greek is much stronger than the modern-day "rubbish." It literally means, "dung." Upon giving his life to Jesus, Paul received a new identity. In order to walk in it he had to die to everything about his old identity. He was not allowed to hold on to any of it.

A year or so after I gave my life to Jesus, God began to heal major portions of my identity. He led me to purge my house of all the objects I had that reminded me of who I was. I threw out shot glasses, pictures, clothes, and music that had become part of my identity. I put everything in a trash bag and took it to the dumpster. When I threw the bag in the dumpster, I declared Galatians 2:20. *Something in me broke!* I'd crossed a line. I was already walking strong in the Lord. My temple was filled. But I had not yet been healed of some things in my wall. After this, my wall was cleansed. Healing came!

What are the objects you need to throw out? This may not be easy for you, but if you truly want to get well you will follow through. Go through your house, your car, and your office and put everything in a trash bag. Throw it out! As you throw it out declare that this person is dead!
Receive this prayer from me on your behalf:

> *"Father, in the name of Jesus, You have taught us that You will forgive us and cleanse us as we confess our sins to You. (Your Name) has confessed their sins in believing lies about who they were. They have renounced them and have embraced who You say they are. In the name of Jesus, they are forgiven!"*

Now, I say to you, "In the name of Jesus, you are forgiven. Walk in your new life!"

Gates: Healing Our Inputs

God restores your gates as you come to Him and allow Him to put His hands on what you allow to enter your city.

- If you have been passive in your thinking, then you need to confess that to the Lord.

    "Father, in the name of Jesus, I confess that I am controlled by my thoughts and not by the Holy Spirit. I entertain thoughts and images that are not of You. I repent of my laziness. I renounce this way of life and reject the lie that it is acceptable. I embrace Your forgiveness and Your way of life. I surrender control of my thoughts to the Holy Spirit. I ask You to train me how to be pro-active in my thoughts and make every thought obedient to Christ."

    Mark a line through this issue. It no longer has control over you.

- If you have been passive in your feeling, then you need to confess that to the Lord.

    "Father, in the name of Jesus, I confess that I am controlled by my emotions instead of the Holy Spirit. I dwell on emotions that are not from You. I confess this has been a way of life for me. I repent! I renounce this way of life and reject the authority it has exercised in me. I embrace Your forgiveness and Your way of life. I surrender control of my life and my emotions to the Holy Spirit. I ask You to train me how to live emotionally appropriate and full in Christ."

    Mark a line through this issue. It no longer has control over you.

- If you have been taking in any form of media that is separating you from the Lord, then now is the time to deal with it. Do not be legalistic. Having strong gates does not mean every bit of music you listen to has to use the name Jesus. But it does mean you need to be mature in the Lord and admit what things you listen to, read, etc. cause you to struggle in the Lord. I have found there are particular songs and TV shows that stir up sin in me. This does not mean I forsake all TV or secular music. It means I am wise in the Lord and reject these particular shows and songs. If it is something you need accountability in, get accountability. (For those battling against internet pornography, Covenant Eyes is an excellent, online accountability tool I have used in the past.) Make your commitment to the Lord. *"Father, in the name of Jesus, I confess I have been watching a TV show that causes me to stumble. I repent of watching this show. I surrender it to You."* If the media you are dealing with can be thrown out, throw it out! Mark a line through this issue. It no longer has control over you.

- If you have been lazy in studying the Bible, then you need to get back to it. Follow the pattern of confession we have already walked through. If the reason you have not been in the Word is because you stay up late and watch TV, then you need to confess that. If the reason you have not been in the Word is because you are too "busy" with work or other things, then you need to confess your idolatry. Ask the Lord to give you guidance in ordering your schedule so that you can meet with Him in the Word.

- If you have been negligent in receiving from the Spirit, then you need to follow the pattern of confession. Allow Him to show you the specific issues you have allowed to distract you from listening to Him.

What we have covered in healing your gates has to do with what you let in your city. What you let out of your city will change as the Spirit heals your temple, walls, and land. So, for example, if you have anger issues and let your anger out of your gates, when your anger is healed in your land then you will no longer let it out of your gates. Let what comes out of your gates reveal what is really in your temple, walls, or land.

As you finish working through your gates, receive this prayer from me:

"Father, in the name of Jesus, You have taught us that you will forgive us and cleanse us as we confess our sins to You. (Your Name) has confessed their sins at their gates. They have renounced them and have embraced Your way of life. Build POWERFUL gates in them! In the name of Jesus, they are forgiven!"

I say to you, "In the name of Jesus, you are forgiven. Be faithful to what God is leading you to do!"

Land: Healing Our Past, Present, and Future

Finally, God moves to restore your land. In freeing your land, God deals with the sins you have committed and the wounds you have incurred.

We are going to work through four examples to show how God heals our land. The first example is a person who has a significant issue with lying that is a generational sin.

The Holy Spirit restores this person by:

- Identifying their sin. Generational sin becomes evident when this person looks at their family history. Because they are aware of generational sin, this is something they consider.

- The person confesses their sin of lying.
- They repent of the specific instances they can recall where they lied. (For someone who has been involved in habitual lying, they will have specific instances they can remember that are significant. The Holy Spirit will also call to mind other instances the person may have forgotten.)

- Then, they renounce their generational connection and reject the authority and control this generational sin has had.

- Finally, they embrace the truth that they have been delivered out of their generational line into the life of Christ, they have been forgiven, and God's will for their lives is honesty. The generational sin of lying has been broken, forgiven, and healed. A new way of life in honesty and truthfulness has opened up as the Holy Spirit enters into this once closed-off area.

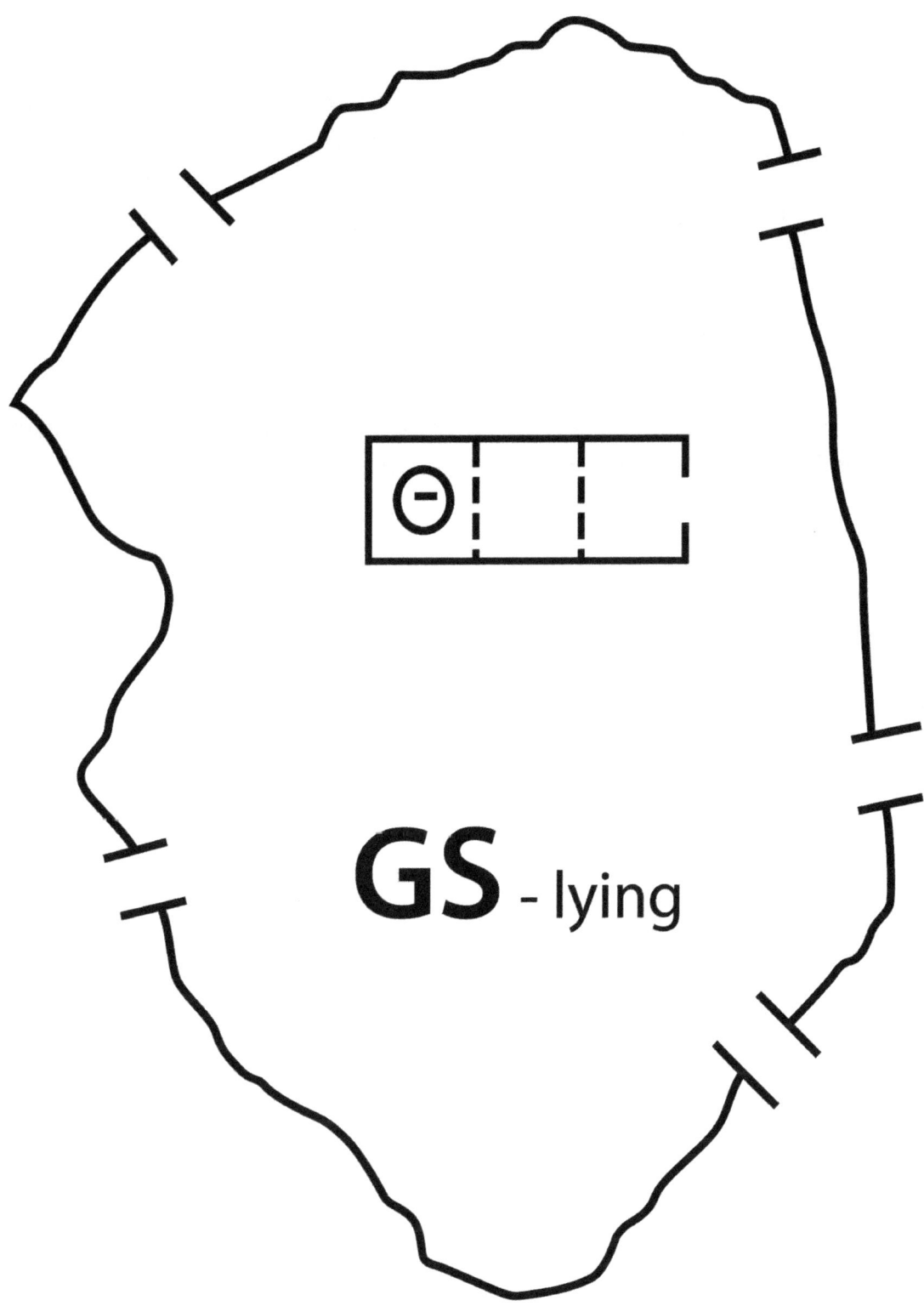

Figure 11: A person who has significant generational sin in the area of lying.

The second example is a person who has suffered significant victimization. This person has chosen to turn to anger and bitterness. In anger, this person has thought and said many destructive things about the person who victimized them. Notice how much of their life is filled with what has been done. None of that space can be filled with the joy of the Lord until this person allows the Spirit access. What is beautiful about this person is that they are now ready to allow Jesus to set them free so that healing can begin! The Holy Spirit comes in, surrounds the area, and lovingly, carefully, begins to lead the person to freedom.

The Holy Spirit frees this person by:

- Comforting them in places and ways no person or words can. As this person turns this to the Lord, they experience the presence of their Father lifting this off of their life.

- In the presence of their Father and the power of the Holy Spirit, the person chooses to forgive whoever has victimized them. Where there are multiple people, the person chooses to forgive each person.

    "Father, in the name of Jesus, I choose to forgive _____ for _____. He/she made me feel _____. In the power of Jesus, I release this person to You and forgive them for what they have done to me."

- Now this person asks God to forgive them for their anger and their judgments.

    "Father, in the name of Jesus, I ask You to forgive me for my anger. Holding on to anger was wrong and it is not of You. Father, forgive me for what I have done. Father, I also ask you to forgive me of the things I have thought and said about this person. Forgive me for these judgments. I release them to You."

- Finally, this person embraces their new condition in the Lord. The victimization no longer defines or controls. This person asks the Holy Spirit to give them a word, picture, or verse of their new condition in Christ. Be still. Listen. Let the Spirit speak. As the Spirit has freed, so too the Spirit will lead in healing and on-going freedom.

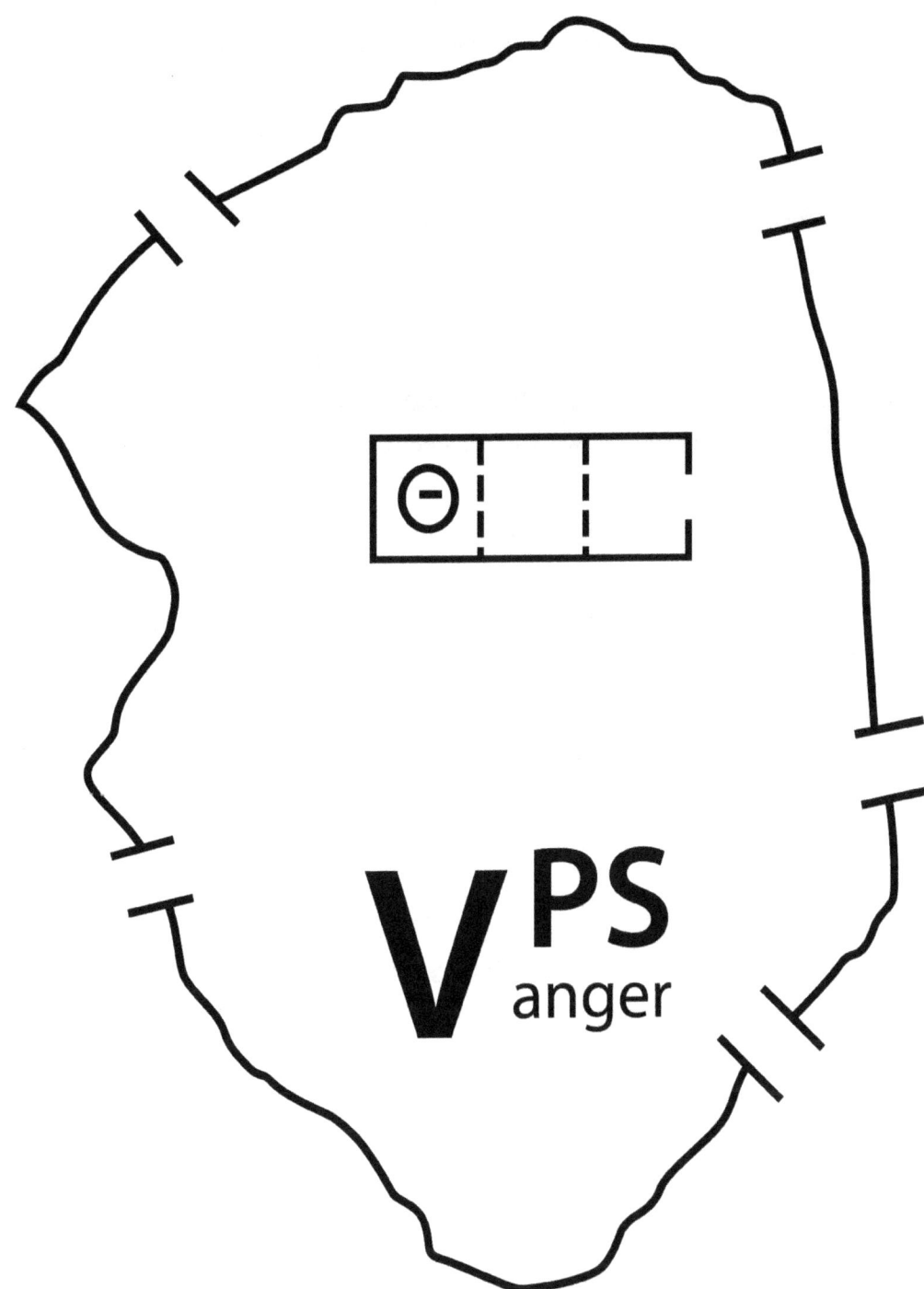

Figure 12: A person suffering from severe victimization who has turned to anger and bitterness.

The third example is a person who has the sin of covetousness in their land that is exacerbated by a worldly lie. Because of their covetousness, they have taken on thousands of dollars in debt. They have used many people in their lives to make themselves look better and have destroyed others with gossip.

The Holy Spirit restores this person by:

- Convicting them of their sin. They are confronted with their greed.

- In their conviction, the person begins to see how they believed a deep, cultural lie that success in life comes through material possessions. The way to feel better is to have the best things. This message has been broadcast through specific magazines, television shows, and websites this person and their friends look at.

- This person, grieved by their own sin, confesses they have lived the sin of covetousness.

- They repent of the specific instances where they have exercised greed. Because their greed led them to tear others down, their repentance leads them to ask God to forgive them for the specific things they have done in tearing down specific people. One person at a time, this person asks God's forgiveness.

- Then, this person renounces the worldly lie they have believed and rejects the authority this lie has had in their lives.

- Finally, this person embraces the truth of God's will that selflessness and giving are the ways of life. The power of this worldly sin has been broken, forgiven, and healing has begun.

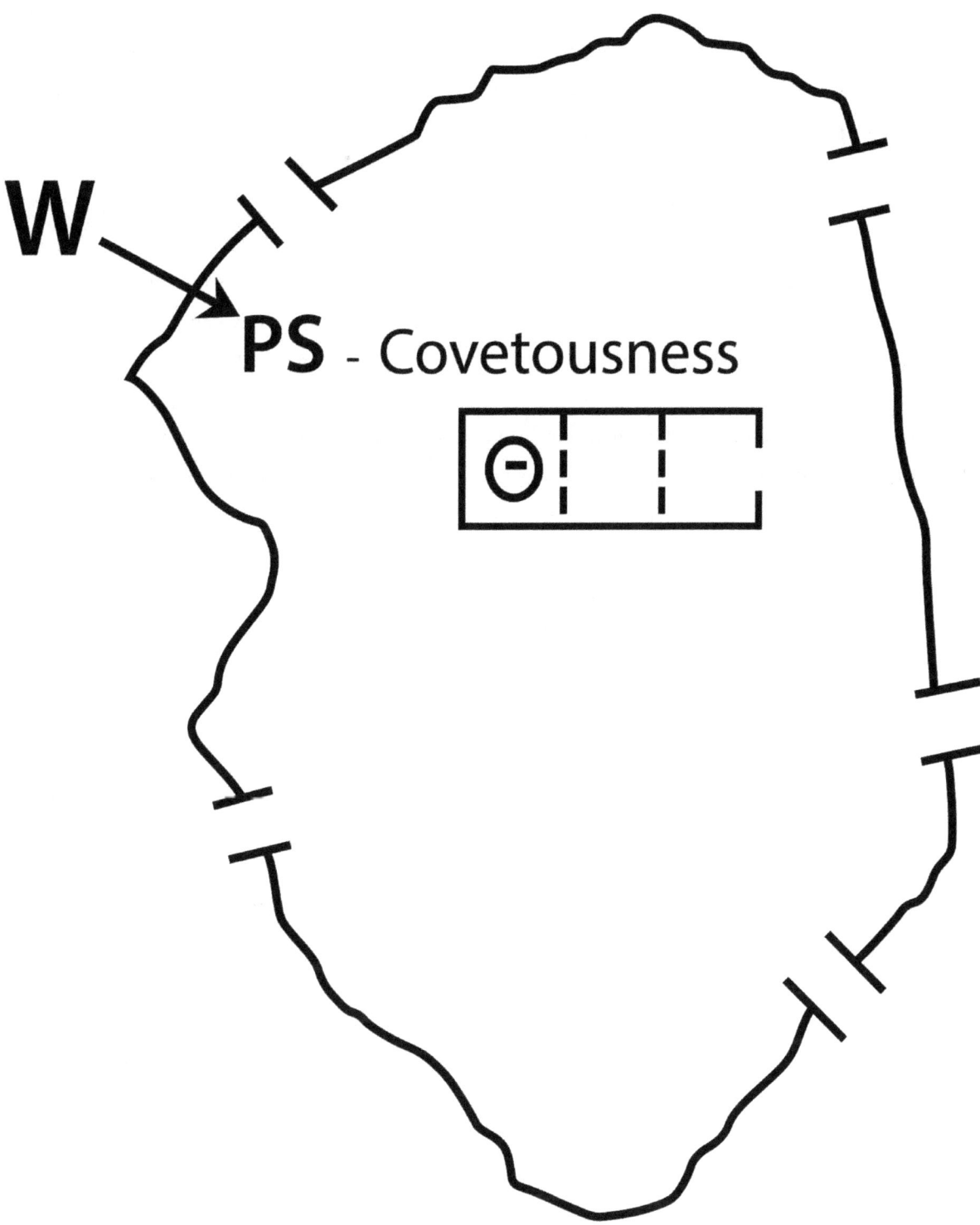

Figure 13: A person struggling with the personal sin of covetousness that originated from a cultural lie.

The fourth example is a person who has the personal sin of immorality compounded by a worldly lie with direct demonic attachment. This person has been very sexually active having sex with many partners. Their entrance into this life was through pornography. After giving their life to Jesus, their mind is still filled with graphic images that bind them.

The Holy Spirit restores this person by:

- Convicting them of the specific sin of immorality. Oftentimes this person will be moved to find freedom because they are exhausted by the continual images they cannot purge. Either way, a person's restoration happens by turning into the issue and dealing with it.

- In considering their sin, the person understands how their path to sin began when they started casually looking at pornography. Their sin was made worse by cultural messages from television, music, and others' lives that promoted sex outside of marriage. Furthermore, the person believes they have some demonic attachment because of the intensity of what is confronting them. Their experience is beyond any kind of illicit hobby. The images are almost debilitating. The accusations are constant. There seems to be no hope and no way through.

- Grieved over their sin, the person confesses their active role in sexual immorality. Because there are other people involved, the person lists the names of those they have been with. The person asks the Father to forgive them in the name of Jesus for each act they committed.

- After receiving forgiveness, the person renounces the worldly lie and the demonic accusations. The person then rejects the demon who has had "ground" in their land. Because the ground has been recaptured, the enemy no longer has a right to be there. He must flee. If the root cause of the demonic attachment was sexual immorality and that sin has been forgiven by the Lord, then the enemy must leave. If sexual immorality is not the root, or there are other roots the enemy has, then those roots will need to be dealt with as well.

- Finally, this person embraces the truth that they are now a child of God, forgiven by the Father. All things old have passed—new things have come. This person embraces the will of God for sexual purity in their lives.

Where you have sexual sin in your land, move through each person on your list asking God to forgive you for what you did with that person. Break all the authority and control that sexual act has had in your life. Renounce it. Pray blessings into that person's life. Mark a line through their names. Repeat this for every person on your list.

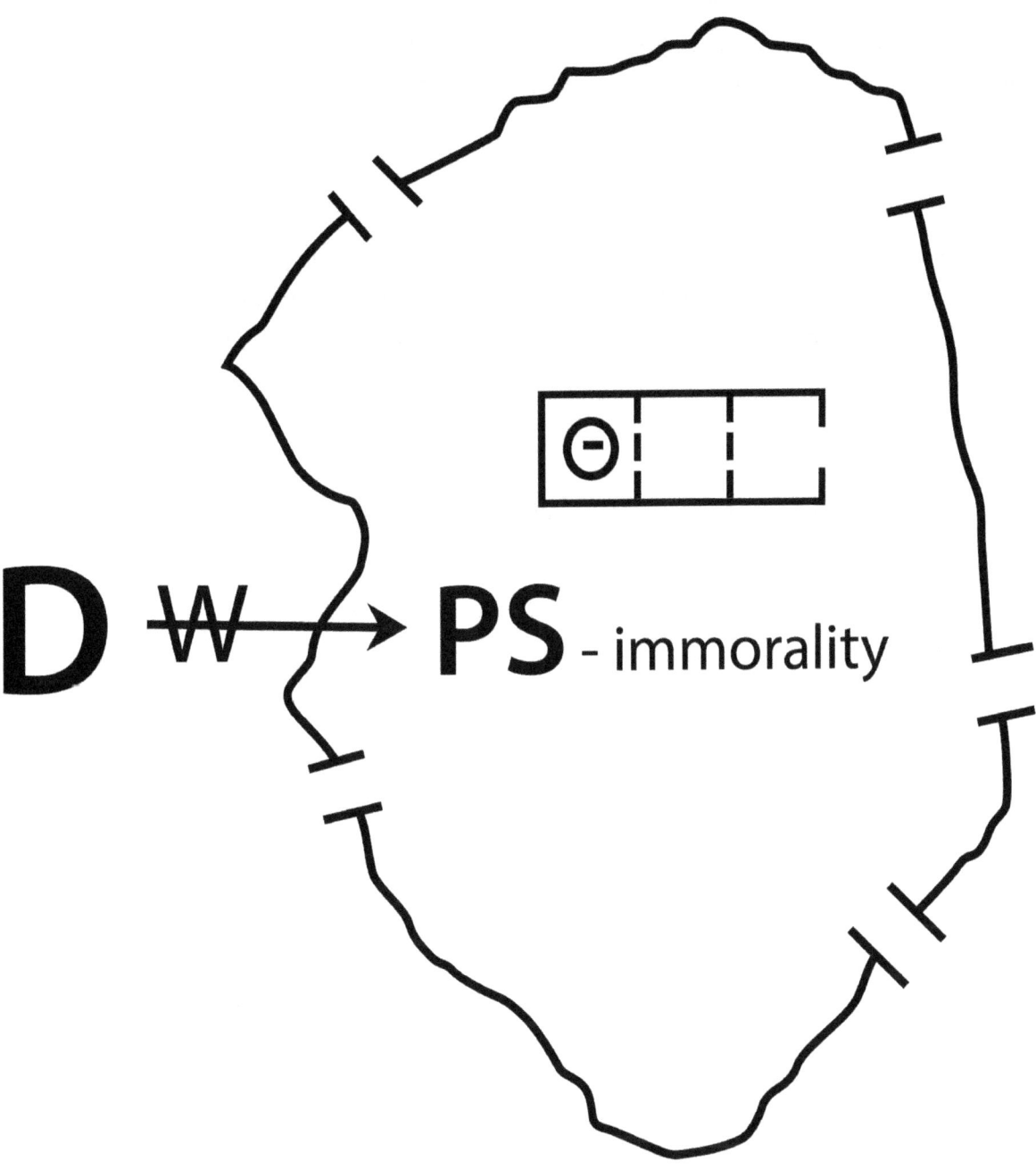

Figure 14: A person who has sexual immorality in their land with direct demonic attachment.

Every one of us has multiple issues in our lands. It is not unusual for a person to have many different demons attached to different issues. Others will have different worldly lies they have believed. Some will have deep wounds that are root causes for other sins that they are battling. Remember, people are messy. Thankfully, the Holy Spirit is working in the authority of Jesus to bring healing, restoration, and transformation to the children of God. Let Him lead. Rest in Him. Let Him speak.

As you conclude your session, take all the papers you have used, crumple them up, throw them out, and declare, "I have been crucified with Christ; and it is no longer I who lives, but Christ who lives in me" (Galatians 2:20). I am no longer this person. I am a child of God and a son/daughter of the King. I am forgiven and filled with His love and purposes for my life!" You should be feeling the Light of Jesus replacing the darkness of sin. Years of burdens have been lifted. Freedom has come!

There are a few other areas we need to cover that will aid our understanding of freedom in Christ.

Body, Emotions, Thoughts, Spirit, Will

Jerusalem's Temple shows that the city was not just a city of bricks and borders. There was more to the city than what anyone could see physically. Jerusalem was also spiritual. The presence of God in the Temple made Jerusalem a city of both the physical and spiritual. We have already seen the intimate connection between the physical and spiritual in Jerusalem. Because the Israelites made idols and lived in sin, God, in the spirit, raised up the Babylonians to decimate the city. There was a direct connection between the physical and the spiritual.

In the same way, you have been made both spirit and body. Genesis 2:7 says, "Then the Lord God formed man of dust from the ground, and breathed into his nostrils the breath of life; and man became a living being." You are far more than what anyone can see, but what can be seen is very important. Contained in your spirit and body are your emotions, thoughts, will, memory, organs, limbs, blood, and everything that makes you you. God has made you so that all of these elements work together *and* affect each other. Your spiritual condition affects your emotions and your emotions affect your spiritual condition. What you eat and how you sleep affect you physically, emotionally, and spiritually.

Therefore, it happens all the time that people are physically fit but miserable in life. They can run a five-minute mile, compete in athletic competitions, or are strikingly beautiful, but they are falling apart internally. Similarly, people can "know the Lord" and be miserable because they do not take care of themselves physically. No matter how much Bible a person can quote, living on fast food and soda with no exercise is going to make a person feel terrible.

When the Holy Spirit comes into a person, He will tend to the whole person. As He challenges what you watch, He will also challenge what you eat. Understanding this may help you discern the source of some of the issues you are battling. For example, if you are suffering from depression, you need to consider what you eat and how you sleep. I have seen people who battle with depression in part because they are physically exhausted but refuse to go to bed before 10:00 pm and refuse to stop eating junk food. I don't care how much Bible you know—poor sleep and diet habits will make you feel terrible.

Self-control may be the last fruit of the Spirit listed in Galatians 5:22–23, but it is still listed! There are others who battle depression because of chemical issues. Just as a person can be born with kidneys that do not operate correctly, so too can a person be born with organs that do not produce the right levels of hormones.

In another example, I have worked with people suffering from high blood pressure who take medication. However, the issue was not biological, it was spiritual. They were experiencing unresolved spiritual oppression from the enemy. Working from a complete perspective of how man is made will open you up to all the possible causes for the bondage you suffer.

This approach does not negate the appropriate use of medicine in the healing process. A person suffering horrific generational depression may need anti-depressants for a season as part of their overall healing. On the other hand, treating depression with anti-depressants and not considering spiritual issues is irresponsible. You need to open yourself in the Lord to all of the possible causes and solutions for the attacks you are under.

If you're seeing a Christian counselor, secular psychiatrist, or some other healthcare professional, ask them what they believe about various potential causes of the issues you have. What options do they consider in healing? If they are missing foundational beliefs about the body/spirit connection in key areas, you may consider asking God to lead you to someone else who is more balanced. Or, you may consider asking God to lead you to someone who is strong in an area where they are weak.

Understanding how God has made you will give you additional wisdom in discerning the source(s) of your issues.

Why God Does Not Heal Everything at Once

It seems like it would be nice if when a person gives their life to Jesus God would instantly heal everything in them. Thankfully, He does not do this. There are at least two reasons God does not work in this way. First, there is no way we can take responsibility for everything we have done at one time. If you give your life to the Lord at thirty, you have lived in sin—a lot of sin—for thirty years. There's no way you're going to take responsibility for everything you've done in the moment you give your life to the Lord.

Secondly, and more importantly, God does not heal everything at once because He wants to teach us how to fight. Judges 3:1 says:

> Now these are the nations which the Lord left, to test Israel by them (that is, all who had not experienced any of the wars of Canaan; only in order that the generations of the sons of Israel might be taught war, those who had not experienced it formerly). These nations are: the five lords of the Philistines and all the Canaanites and the Sidonians and the Hivites who lived in Mount Lebanon, from Mount Baal-hermon as far as Lebo-hamath. They were for testing Israel, to find out if they would obey the commandments of the Lord, which He had commanded their fathers through Moses.

A new generation of Israel was in the land. They had not experienced any of the wars of their fathers. However, the Lord knew that war was a part of living in a fallen world. Instead of taking out all of their enemies, the Lord left some for Israel to deal with so that they could learn how to fight.

Even though we are saved, we are still living in a world at war. The enemy, lies of the world, and sin are still active. God will use the things we are still dealing with to train us how to fight. To be free and to live in freedom is to fight!

Freedom Session

A freedom session should take several hours. This is a dedicated time where a person is seeking to get cleaned out of many different areas of their lives. These are most effective when led by someone who has experience in their own freedom as well as helping others. Freedom sessions can happen in one day, over a weekend, or in a series of sessions. The emphasis in these sessions is freedom and restoration. The emphasis is not on extended counseling.

In a freedom session a person will be able to deal with many different issues in their cities. By following what has been outlined using the attached worksheets and following the leading of the Holy Spirit, a person can deal with many areas of bondage in their life. However, it is always better to go through this with others leading. If your church has a freedom or counseling ministry, ask them if they can help you walk through this.

The greatest influence in a person's freedom is their willingness to allow the Holy Spirit to deal with their issues. Everything has to be open. In John 5 Jesus was in Jerusalem. He came upon a man who had been ill for *thirty-eight years*. Jesus asked him a bizarre question in John 5:6, "Do you wish to get well?" What an odd question to ask one who has been sick for thirty-eight years. However, Jesus knew that many people get comfortable in their sickness. They can build an identity around their condition in many different ways. Jesus knew that this man had to want to get well to get well. Thankfully, the man said, "Yes." Jesus healed him.

Before you consider working through your city, "Do you wish to get well?"

Staying Free

Paul writes in Galatians 5:1, "It was for freedom you have been set free; therefore keep standing firm and do not be subject again to a yoke of slavery." It is one thing to be set free. It is another to live free. Jesus warns us against getting free and then returning to our old ways of life.

> Now when the unclean spirit goes out of a man, it passes through waterless places seeking rest, and does not find it. Then it says, "I will return to my house from which I came"; and when it comes, it finds it unoccupied, swept, and put in order. Then it goes and takes along with it seven other spirits more wicked than itself, and they go in and live there; and the last state of that man becomes worse than the first (Matthew 12:43–45),

A person does not get freed so that they can go back to whatever life they were living before. To be freed is to live life in a completely new way. *The Holy Spirit will teach you how to live free.* As the Holy Spirit enters into areas of darkness, He brings light. That light transforms and changes people. How we think, feel, spend our time, believe, and act all begin to change as light takes over more and more of our cities.

One effective exercise to walk in freedom you can practice immediately is soaking, also called meditating, abiding, or reflecting. I like "soaking" because it gives the picture of resting in or being absorbed in something. Soak in the Holy Spirit and the Word of God. This is not about Scripture memory or Bible study necessarily. This is about being gripped by one truth of the Lord and soaking in it. For example, you may be moved to soak in the faithfulness of God. All day you are thinking about, writing about, and resting in the faithfulness of God. Allow the Holy Spirit to take the faithfulness of your Father deeper and deeper into you. Give Him freedom to do what He wants in you as you are immersed in Him.

There are many other ways in which the Holy Spirit will teach you how to live freely including:

- Developing a healthy prayer life
- Studying and memorizing the Scripture
- Serving the Lord by following the Spirit to help those He calls us to
- Sharing Jesus with others
- Exercising other practices of the faith like worship, fasting, journaling, and silence
- Joining a body of Christ and being baptized

It is also very advantageous to learn a particular way of walking in relationship with the Father, Son, and Holy Spirit. Walking in a specific way will give you the structure you need so that you can succeed in the Lord. *The Way of Rest*, another workbook of mine, presents one such method. Based on Jesus's promise in Matthew 11:28, "Come to Me all who are weary and heavy-laden and I will give you rest," *The Way of Rest* provides a structure whereby you will learn how to live in the promised rest of Jesus. You can learn this method by reading the book *The Way of Rest*.

The best way to learn the Way of Rest, or any other method of walking with Jesus, is to be personally discipled. Personal discipleship is the way Jesus trained His main followers. He spent most of His time pouring Himself into twelve men. If your church offers people who will disciple you, take advantage of it. If not, pray and ask our Father to send someone into your life who can love you and train you in how to walk with the Lord.

Fasting, Freedom, and Staying Free

With respect to freedom, fasting is the ultimate weapon God has given us. There are a few different types of fasts. The one that is relevant to freedom is spending a day or more without eating any food. During that day you will drink plenty of water and take extra time to rest in the presence of God. When you are fasting for the purposes of freedom, it will be important to fast regularly. Fasting once is not going to work.

In issues of bondage, we are confronting areas of our lives—thought patterns, emotional patterns, behavior choices—that are ingrained. We do not feel like we have control of them. Through fasting God equips us by the Holy Spirit with the indispensable gift of self-control. Other than air there is no more basic need that you have than food. During a regular day, when you get hungry you eat. You have unknowingly become a slave to your physical appetite. Fasting teaches you how to exercise self-control over food. God will show you that once you are equipped to deny your physical need for food that taking control over your thoughts, emotions, and other behaviors will be much easier.

Fasting is a powerful weapon when dealing with "inescapable" images. Sin, the world, and Satan are masterful at using all sorts of images in your mind. When you are not used to taking every thought captive, image warfare can be a very effective tool against you. Fasting teaches you how to live out of the surpassing power of the Holy Spirit to deny even the most graphic of imagery.

Our Father used fasting as one of the weapons of choice in healing me of pornography usage. In addition to confronting my walls and my land, God taught me to fast. I had years of illicit images catalogued in my mind. Through fasting I was trained to deny these. They went away! Before fasting I did not know that was possible.

Isaiah 58 is the classic text on fasting. In the passage, bad fasting is contrasted with proper, godly fasting. In verse 6 God says, "Is this not the fast which I choose, to loosen the bonds of wickedness, to undo the bands of the yoke, and to let the oppressed go free and break every yoke?" Fasting is for loosening bonds and breaking yokes. God says in verse 8 that when we fast properly, "Then your light will break out like the dawn, and your recovery will speedily spring forth; and your righteousness will go before you; the glory of the Lord will be your rear guard."

Depending on what you are dealing with, you may need to fast as a way of freedom and continuing to walk in freedom. A typical day of fasting is not eating food for a calendar day. Here is a short list of fasting dos and don'ts:

- Do spend extra time resting in the presence of God listening to Him.

- Do drink plenty of water.

- Don't beat yourself up if you do not make it. Learn to fast. If you do not make it, praise the Lord for the step you have taken and ask Him to lead you again the next time.

- Don't stay up late. I find people will lose their day because they stayed up late, got weak, and ate. Go to bed early. It is not unusual to get weak toward the end of the day.

- Do expect your stomach to scream! It's throwing a temper tantrum. For all of your life, whenever it's complained, you've eaten. Now you're denying your stomach. You are not going to die!

- Do consult your doctor before fasting if you have any concerns whatsoever.

- Do quit caffeine two to three days before fasting. Fasting is hard enough as it is without having to battle caffeine withdrawals while you're doing it. If you cannot quit two to three days before, consider taking some aspirin or other pain reliever in the morning.

- Do not brag about fasting. If you're married, your spouse certainly needs to know you're fasting. Know that fasting does not make you anything special. It certainly does not make you a super Christian. If someone finds out, or if you have to tell someone for work reasons, it's not a big deal. You do not "lose credit."

- Do be open to the Lord leading you to fast longer than one day. It is normal for people to fast three to five days. God calls some to fast for forty days. If you feel like the Lord is calling you to an extended fast, I recommend you read some books that will give you specific direction or talk to someone who has experience.

- Do be in for the long haul. You will not get healed or develop self-control in one fast. Allow God to draw you deeper into Him. Rest in Him. Let Him show you whatever He wants. No matter what you do in your fast, always seek greater intimacy with God. Even more than freedom, seek intimacy.

As you go through fasting, prayerfully the discipline will become a regular part of your life. As Jesus taught us to pray, He teaches us to fast. Fasting is not only a fantastic weapon in freedom, it is also a beautiful tool for ongoing, deepening intimacy.

Ongoing Healing

Healing in the Lord is a lifelong process that happens as you walk with the Father, Son, and Holy Spirit. They are never done ministering to you. A freedom session like this will be a significant step forward in your transformation. However, your transformation will not be complete until you are called home. Rest in Him knowing He is at work in you. No one is perfect. No one is beyond the healing and freeing work of God.

Oftentimes, God breaks the control of our issues as the first step in the healing process. Now that bondage has been broken, the Holy Spirit begins to heal. For example, if you have been living under the darkness of demonic depression and it is broken, then the Holy Spirit floods that part of your city and you begin to learn how to live in joy. If you have been bound to pornographic thoughts, Jesus will shatter that bond and the Holy Spirit will teach you how to live anew. Healing is a process. Be careful of believing the lie that now you have it all figured out and no longer need God to minister to you!

Conclusion

Your freedom is the will of the Father, the mission of the Son, and the work of the Holy Spirit. The city of your life has been under siege for years. Today is the day God wants to free you! Today is the day God wants to heal you—throwing off every source of bondage that has weighed you down. You no longer have to live this way. Victory is yours in Jesus Christ.

It may be painful and difficult to look at the reality of your city. However, God is amazing in His ability to walk you through whatever He wants to address. Let Him lead you. Take each step with Him. Do not live one more day in bondage. Jesus died to set you free!

May the Holy Spirit clearly show you what He is doing in you. And, as you get healed, may He powerfully send you to help others walk in the freedom you have.

Appendix 1: List of Sins

Some of the lists of sin found in the Scripture are:

Exodus 20:1–17
1. Other gods
2. Idolatry
3. Blasphemy
4. Unfaithfulness
5. Dishonoring parents
6. Murder
7. Adultery
8. Stealing
9. Lying
10. Greed/Covetousness

Proverbs 6:16–20
1. Pride
2. Lying
3. Murder
4. Heart that devises wicked plans
5. False witness
6. Divisiveness

Matthew 5–7
1. Anger
2. Adultery
3. Divorce
4. Breaking your word
5. Revenge
6. Love of money
7. Anxiety
8. Judgmentalism
9. Rebellion

Romans 1:26–32
1. Homosexuality
2. Unrighteousness
3. Wickedness
4. Greed
5. Evil
6. Envy
7. Murder
8. Dissention
9. Deceit
10. Nastiness
11. Gossip
12. Slander
13. Hating God
14. Rude
15. Arrogance
16. Boastful
17. Disobedient to parents
18. Untrustworthy
19. Unloving
20. Unmerciful

Galatians 5:19–21
1. Immorality
2. Impurity
3. Sensuality
4. Idolatry
5. Sorcery
6. Hostilities
7. Strife
8. Jealousy
9. Outbursts of anger
10. Disputes
11. Dissention
12. Factions
13. Envy
14. Drunkenness
15. Carousing

Appendix 2: Names God Calls Me

Citizens of the Kingdom – Mark 1:15
Fisher of men – Mark 1:17
Student – Luke 6:40
Follower – Luke 9:23
Born Again – John 1:12–13
Free – John 8:31

Soldier – Philippians 2:3
Saint – Colossians 1:2
Holy – Colossians 3:12
Beloved – Colossians 3:12
Servant of Jesus – James 1:1

More than conqueror – Romans 8:37
Temples of the Holy Spirit – 1 Corinthians 6:19–20
New Creation – 2 Corinthians 5:17
Sons and Daughters of the Father – Galatians 4:1–7

Forgiven – 1 John 1:7
Beloved child of God – 1 John 3:1
Overcomer – 1 John 5:4

Ephesians 1:1–13
Blessed
Chosen
Predestined
Redeemed
Sealed

1 Peter 2:9–10
Chosen Race
Royal Priesthood
Holy Nation
A People for God's Own Possession
People of God

Appendix 3: Freedom Worksheet

Use this worksheet to get free from the issues God wants to deal with in the four areas of your life.

Enemies

Sin – Garden, Generational, Personal (vows, victimization, sexual, others)
The World – Culture/sub-culture, Gender, Education, Government, Religion, Others
Satan - Temptation, Oppression, Attachment, Possession

Freedom

Confess – Accept responsibility for your actions.
Repent – Turn from what you were doing to the way of the Lord.
Renounce – Declare that what you were doing is a lie.
Reject – In the name of Jesus, cast off all authority and control that sin, the world, and Satan have exercised in you through this lie.
Embrace – Accept God's new truth for you in each area He is addressing.

For example:

Heavenly Father, I confess that I have been sexually immoral with _____. I repent of this sin. Please forgive me. I renounce the worldly and demonic lie that sex before marriage is acceptable. In the name of Jesus, I command this demon spirit of perversion to leave me right now. You no longer have authority in my life. Holy Father, I embrace Your forgiveness and the way of holiness You have for me.

Temple

In the temple section, list the issues you have with the Father, Son, and Holy Spirit. If you have a "blocking" issue(s), then list that in the left column. If you have Trinitarian imbalance, list that in the left column as well. Then mark the sources of those issues. If your blocking issue is riches, then you mark personal sin of greed and the world – cultural lie.

TEMPLE	Victimization	The World	Satan

Pray and ask the Holy Spirit to show you any other issues in your temple that He wants to address. If they do not "fit" the chart, list them here:

1. _____

2. _____

3. _____

For each item in the table and on your list, go through the freedom process. Confess, repent, renounce, reject, and embrace. As you move through each item, make a line through it!

Walls

In the walls section, list the ungodly names you have taken on in the left column. Then list the source(s) of the name. For example, if the name came from your dad, then in the victimization column write, "Dad." A name can have multiple sources. When you choose to believe a lie in your walls, you become guilty of unbelief. Make sure you mark your responsibility for each name.

WALLS	Victimization	Sin	The World	Satan	God's Name

Remember that your identity can also be associated with items you have in your home or other places. What are the items God is leading you to throw away?

_____   _____   _____   _____

_____   _____   _____   _____

Pray and ask the Holy Spirit to show you any other issues in your walls that He wants to address. For those that do not "fit" the chart, list them here:

1. _____

2. _____

3. _____

For each item, go through the freedom process as you did in your temple. When you finish each line, mark a line through it.

Land

In your land, list the sins you have committed. Where you have unforgiveness and/or sexual sins, you may need to use a separate sheet of paper to list those you are angry with and/or have been sexually active with. You may write "sexual" in the sin column and then work through each person on a separate sheet of paper. If your sin has been fueled by the world or demonic involvement, then mark that appropriately.

LAND	Victimization	Sin	The World	Satan

Pray and ask the Holy Spirit to show you any other issues in your walls that He wants to address. For those that do not "fit" the chart, list them here:

1. _____

2. _____

3. _____

For each item go, through the freedom process as you did in your temple. When you finish each line, mark a line through it.

Gates

How do your gates need to be restored? Do you have sin God wants to deal with in what you have been watching or listening to? Is your Father showing you that you have ungodly thought/emotional habits? List your gate issues. If they have been fueled by the world or Satan, note that appropriately.

GATES	Victimization	Sin	The World	Satan

Pray and ask the Holy Spirit to show you any other issues in your gates that He wants to address. For any issues that do not "fit" in the table, list them here:

1. _____

2. _____

3. _____

For each item, go through the freedom process as you did in your temple. When you finish each line, mark a line through it.

Congratulations on your freedom! Ask the Holy Spirit to show you what your city looks like now. Ask Him to give you a word, a picture, or a verse of God's love for you.

This is who you are! This is what Jesus died on the cross to do in you!

Now, live freely. Embrace a way of walking in the Lord. Pray for discipleship. Join a church. Rest in Him and His Word. Let the Holy Spirit lead you every day!

"It was for freedom that Christ set us free; therefore keep standing firm and do not be subject again to a yoke of slavery."

— The Apostle Paul, Galatians 5:1

FURTHER READING

Spiritual Warfare, Healing, and Freedom

Bondage Breaker, Neal Anderson

Deep Wounds Deep Healing, Charles Kraft

Defeating Dark Angels, Charles Kraft

Deliverance and Inner healing, John and Mark Sandford

Discipleship Counseling, Neal Anderson

The Gift of Forgiveness, Charles Stanley

The Handbook to Happiness, Charles R. Solomon

The Invisible War, Donald Grey Barnhouse

Spiritual Warfare, Karl Payne (An excellent read for dealing with demonic issues.)

The Strategies of Satan, Warren Wiersbe

The Three Battlegrounds, Francis Frangipane

Transforming the Inner Man, John and Paula Sandford

The Wounded Heart: Hope for Adult Victims of Childhood Sexual Abuse, Dan Allender

Discipleship Method

The Way of Rest, Jim Stern

ABOUT THE AUTHOR

Jim Stern is a pastor, speaker, consultant, and author.

He leads CORE, a disciple-making movement in Houston, Texas, and founded Trexo, a discipleship consulting ministry.

He has written two other books, *The On Ramp* and *Be: The Way of Rest*, the first of the three-part *Be, Go, Make* series. He will release *Oneness: Seven Lessons on Marriage from the Garden of Eden* in 2016.

Jim lives in Houston, Texas, with his wife, Brooke, and his two kids, Collin and Claire. In addition to his love of authentically walking with Jesus and restoring people, Jim trains in Brazilian jiu-jitsu.

Visit his ministries at Corehouston.org and Trexo.org.